# 100 Quickwrites

### Fast and Effective Freewriting Exercises That Build Students' Confidence, Develop Their Fluency, and Bring Out the Writer in Every Student

by Linda Rief

SCHOLASTIC
**Teaching**
*Resources*

NEW YORK ● TORONTO ● LONDON ● AUCKLAND ● SYDNEY
MEXICO CITY ● NEW DELHI ● HONG KONG ● BUENOS AIRES

Every effort has been made to find the authors and publishers of the poems in this book and obtain permission to print them. Thank you to the students whose work appears in this collection. p. 20, "That Girl" by Gary Soto. From *New and Selected Poems* by Gary Soto. Copyright © 1995 by Gary Soto. Used with permission of Chronicle Books LLC, San Francisco. Visit www.chroniclebooks.com; p. 21, "Time Somebody Told Me" by Quantedius Hall. Copyright © 2000 by Quantedius Hall. From *You Hear Me?*, edited by Betsy Franco, published by Candlewick Press; p. 24 and 40, "Waiting for the Splash" and "Owl Pellets" by Ralph Fletcher. From *I Am Wings* by Ralph Fletcher. Copyright © 1994 by Ralph Fletcher. Used by permission of Marian Reiner for the author; p. 27, "He Shaved His Head" by Rene Ruiz. Copyright © 2000 by Rene Ruiz. From *You Hear Me?*, edited by Betsy Franco, published by Candlewick Press; p. 29, "Insanity" by Gaston Dubois. From *American Sports Poems*, collected by May Swenson and R. R. Knudson, published by Orchard Books, 1988; p. 33, "Hockey" by Scott Blaine is reprinted from *Grab Me a Bus. . . and Other Award Winning Poems* by Malcolm Glass and M. Joe Eaton. Copyright © 1974 by Scholastic Magazines, Inc. Reprinted by permission of Scholastic Inc.; p. 36, "Swinging the River" by Charles Harper Webb. From *Preposterous*, copyright © 1991 by Paul Janeczko. Published by Orchard Books; p. 38, "Ringside" by Ron Koetge. From *Heart to Heart*, edited by Jan Greenberg, copyright © 2001 by Harry N. Abrams, Inc; p. 42, 54, and 61, "Edge of Life," "The Sadness Tree," and "If Only," by Abigail Lynne Becker from *A Box of Rain*. *A Box of Rain* is an anthology of original artwork, poetry, and photography. Orders ($10 per book) can be placed at rbantique@aol.com. Address requests to Linda Becker (Abigail's mom); p. 48, "Mama Sewing" by Eloise Greenfield and Lessie Jones Little. From *Childtimes: A Three-Generation Memoir*; p. 50, "To a Daughter Leaving Home" by Linda Pastan. From *Carnival Evening*, copyright © 1988 by Linda Pastan. Published by W. W. Norton & Co.; p. 55, 62, and 112, "Franz Dominquez," "Norman Moskowitz," and "Eleanor Paine" by Mel Glenn. From *Class Dismissed!* Copyright © 1982 by Mel Glenn; p. 56, "Where I Live" by Wesley McNair. From *The Faces of Americans in 1853* by Wesley McNair (University of Missouri Press). Copyright (c) 1983 by Wesley McNair. Reprinted by permission of Wesley McNair; p. 58, "My Sky" by Sharon Creech. From *Love That Dog*, copyright © 2001 by Sharon Creech. Published by HarperCollins Children's Books, a division of HarperCollins Publishers; p. 77, "Knoxville, Tennessee" by Nikki Giovanni. From *Knoxville, Tennessee*, copyright © 1968, 1970 by Nikki Giovanni, published by Scholastic; p. 83, "Autumn" by Linda Pastan. From *Heroes in Disguise*, copyright © 1991 by Linda Pastan. Published by W.W. Norton & Co.; p. 84, "Buttermints" by Amity Gaige. Copyright © 1990 by Amity Gaige. From the published book, *We Are a Thunderstorm*, Landmark Editions, Inc.; p. 100, "Embassy" by W.H. Auden; p. 101, "The Game" by Myra Cohn Livingston. Copyright © 1990 by Myra Cohn Livingston. Used by permission of Marian Reiner. Appeared originally in *The Big Book for Peace*; p. 102, "Dear Mr. President" by Naomi Shihab Nye. Reprinted with permission of Simon & Schuster Books for Young Readers, an imprint of Simon & Schuster Children's Publishing Division from *Sitti's Secrets* by Naomi Shihab Nye. Text copyright © 1994 by Naomi Shihab Nye; p. 108, "Writing Past Midnight" by Alice Schertle. From *A Lucky Thing* by Alice Schertle. Copyright © 1999, 1997 by Alice Shertle, reprinted by permission of Harcourt, Inc.; p. 109, "But I'll Be Back Again" by Cynthia Rylant. Excerpts from *But I'll Be Back Again*, copyright © 1989 by Cynthia Rylant, published by Orchard Books; p. 111, "Available Light" by Mekeel McBride. Reprinted from *Red Letter Days* by permission of Carnegie Mellon University Press. Copyright © 1988 by Mekeel McBride; p. 113, "After English Class" by Jean Little. From *Hey World, Here I Am!* Copyright © 1986 by Jean Little. Kids Can Press Ltd.; p. 115, "My Grandmother's Hair" by Cynthia Rylant. Copyright © 1991 by Cynthia Rylant. From *To Ride a Butterfly*. Copyright © 1991 by Bantam Doubleday Dell Publishing Group, Inc.

Pieces first published in *Seeking Diversity: Language Arts with Adolescents* by Linda Rief (Heinemann: Portsmouth, NH, 1992): "The Nursing Home," "School Daze," "A Day in July," "Fog," "Black River," "Through the Night Window," "And I'm Not Ready," "Old," "Great Grandfather," "To Seabrook." Pieces first published in *Vision and Voice* by Linda Rief (Heinemann: Portsmouth, NH, 1999): "Liver!," "I'd Rather," "Jen," "Days at the Farmhouse."

Cover design by James Sarfati
Interior design by Sarah Morrow

Copyright © 2003 by Linda Rief
All rights reserved. Published by Scholastic Inc.
Printed in the U.S.A.
ISBN 0-439-45877-3
8  9  10    40    09  08  07  06

# Table of Contents

Foreword . . . . . . . . . . . . . . . . . . . . . 5

Introduction . . . . . . . . . . . . . . . . . . . 7

  What Is a Quickwrite? . . . . . . . . . . . . . 8

  The Benefits of Quickwrites. . . . . . . . . . . 8

  Teaching With Quickwrites . . . . . . . . . . . 10

  Objective of This Book. . . . . . . . . . . . . 11

  Choosing Models for Quickwrites . . . . . . . . 11

  Taking Quickwrites Further . . . . . . . . . . . 14

  Leading Students to Literacy . . . . . . . . . . 15

  Professional Resources for Quickwrites. . . . . . 16

100 Models for Quickwrites

  A Slice of Life  *Katherine T.* . . . . . . . . . . . 17

  Dandelions  *Graeham D.* . . . . . . . . . . . . . 18

  Jen  *Jeff B.* . . . . . . . . . . . . . . . . . . . . . 19

  That Girl  *Gary Soto* . . . . . . . . . . . . . . . 20

  Time Somebody Told Me  *Quantedius Hall* . . . . 21

  Within  *Lindsay H.* . . . . . . . . . . . . . . . . 22

  Moon Mission: To-Do List  *Samuel L.* . . . . . . 23

  Waiting for the Splash  *Ralph Fletcher* . . . . . . 24

  School Daze  *Jay S.* . . . . . . . . . . . . . . . . 25

  Just Me, the Ball, and the Basket  *Dipta B.* . . . . 26

  He Shaved His Head  *Rene Ruiz* . . . . . . . . . 27

  A Day in July  *Janet M.* . . . . . . . . . . . . . 28

  Insanity  *Gaston Dubois*. . . . . . . . . . . . . . 29

  Rambling Autobiography  *Linda Rief* . . . . . . . 30

  Liver!  *Jim B.* . . . . . . . . . . . . . . . . . . . 31

  First Television  *Heejung K.* . . . . . . . . . . . . 32

  Hockey  *Scott Blaine*. . . . . . . . . . . . . . . . 33

  When She Was Fifteen  *Linda Rief* . . . . . . . . 34

Flaws?  *Owen A.*. . . . . . . . . . . . . . . . . . 35

Swinging the River  *Charles Harper Webb*. . . . . 36

When I Was Young at the Ocean
  *Linda Rief*. . . . . . . . . . . . . . . . . . . . 37

Ringside  *Ron Koertge* . . . . . . . . . . . . . . 38

Syncros Hinged Mountain Head Stem
  *Trapper S.* . . . . . . . . . . . . . . . . . . . 39

Owl Pellets  *Ralph Fletcher* . . . . . . . . . . . 40

I need to find a place  *Emily G.* . . . . . . . . . 41

Edge of Life  *Abigail Lynne Becker* . . . . . . . . 42

Hibiscus  *Graeham D.* . . . . . . . . . . . . . . 43

Petrified gray face  *Erica S., Kira G., Jordan S.* . . 44

My mother always wanted  *Heejung K.* . . . . . . 45

The Hole in My Suit  *Danielle M.* . . . . . . . . 46

Nail Biting  *Emma T.* . . . . . . . . . . . . . . . 47

Mama Sewing  *Eloise Greenfield and
  Lessie Jones Little.* . . . . . . . . . . . . . . . 48

Audition  *Emily A.*. . . . . . . . . . . . . . . . . 49

To a Daughter Leaving Home
  *Linda Pastan* . . . . . . . . . . . . . . . . . 50

On Being Asked to Select the Most
  Memorable Day in My Life  *Rebecca K.* . . . . 51

Without Its Stones…  *Caitlin F.* . . . . . . . . . 52

She Thinks I Don't Know  *Alison A.* . . . . . . . 53

The Sadness Tree  *Abigail Lynne Becker* . . . . . 54

Franz Dominquez  *Mel Glenn* . . . . . . . . . . 55

Where I Live  *Wesley McNair* . . . . . . . . . . . 56

And I'm Not Ready  *Stacey S.*. . . . . . . . . . . 57

Split Second  *Steve L.*. . . . . . . . . . . . . . . 58

Socrates  *Ming-Hui F.* . . . . . . . . . . . . . . 59

Days at the Farmhouse *Kirsten J.* .............. 60

If Only *Abigail Lynne Becker* .................. 61

Norman Moskowitz *Mel Glenn* .............. 62

On Visiting My Great-Aunt Who Lived in
    a Three-Decker in Dorchester *Linda Rief*....63

Remembrance: For My Grandmother
    *Lindsay O.* ................................. 64

What is it about my Grandpa? *Hannah L.* ..... 65

He is my Great-Grandfather *Toby M.*.......... 66

Don't You See *Zack S.* ......................... 67

Fear *Ben H.* .................................... 68

Old *Matt F.* ................................... 69

Early Risers *Marianne S.*....................... 70

The Nursing Home *Karen G.* ................. 71

Penny *Kerri B.* ................................ 72

Cooling Out *Rebecca K.*........................ 73

Released *Natasha P.*............................ 74

My Sky *Sharon Creech*......................... 75

What the Pony Taught Us *Martha B. Kane* ..... 76

Knoxville, Tennessee *Nikki Giovanni* ......... 77

P.S. 81 The Bronx *Naomi S.*.................... 78

The Dunes *Jeremy G.* ......................... 79

Watermelon Day *Rebecca K.*................... 80

Fog *Janet M.* .................................. 81

School Days *Trisha W.*.......................... 82

Autumn *Linda Pastan* ......................... 83

Buttermints *Amity Gaige* ...................... 84

Walking Down a Stone Driveway *Dana S.*...... 85

Through the Night Window I Imagine
    What Could Be Hidden *Nahanni R.* ........ 86

Black River *Janet M.* ........................... 87

February Air *Paula M.* .......................... 88

And Spring Whispers Utopia *Abigail C.*........ 89

Crossing the River *Jesse S.* ..................... 90

Unknown Soldier *Duncan H.* .................. 91

Charlotte's Web *Lindsay O.*.................... 92

Only Human *Kerri B.*.......................... 93

The White Flakes (On Reading
    *Schindler's List*) *Ben W.*..................... 94

Reverence *Lindsay O.*.......................... 95

Seabrook Nuclear Power Plant
    To Whom It May Concern: *Sandy P.* ........ 96

A Hollow Smile *Dave H.* ...................... 97

Little Boys *Emma T.*........................... 98

And So It Goes *Duncan H.*..................... 99

Embassy *W. H. Auden* ......................... 100

The Game *Myra Cohn Livingston*.............. 101

Dear Mr. President *Naomi Shihab Nye* ....... 102

Tragedy Strikes Columbine *Kristen C.*......... 103

September 11, 2001. . . *Hannah L.* ........... 104

Simple Truths *Anupama V.*.................... 105

Let Me Introduce Myself *Megan G.* ........... 106

Poetry Was . . . *Al Mahmud/Linda Rief*....... 107

Writing Past Midnight *Alice Schertle*.......... 108

But I'll Be Back Again *Cynthia Rylant*........ 109

I'd Rather . . . *Adam B.*....................... 110

Available Light *Mekeel McBride* .............. 111

Eleanor Paine *Mel Glenn* ..................... 112

After English Class *Jean Little* ................ 113

Reading *Juliana M. and Ben R.* ............... 114

My Grandmother's Hair *Cynthia Rylant*....... 115

The Unwritten Pages *Megan G.* .............. 116

Building From the Quickwrites.................... **117**

# Foreword

Linda Rief knows that there is nothing more powerful than writing. "Writing is thinking," she says; when we write we discover meaning in the world around us and in our own lives. She has always had high expectations of her students, of other teachers, and, most of all, of herself. She insists that her eighth graders write every day in multiple genres and for multiple purposes, urging that we who teach writing also write, and leading by her own example. For 20 years she has been sharing her classroom expertise at national and regional conferences and at writers' institutes and workshops across the country. Thousands of teachers credit her with turning them into writers.

People can be a little phobic about writing, and teachers are no exception. We fear revealing ourselves on the page. We are sure we have nothing of value to say. We worry about sounding trivial or self-absorbed. So, how can we move beyond our fears? How can we dive in and experience the surprise and discovery that leads to new insight and new knowledge? One of the most compelling ways Linda has helped students, both adolescent and adult, take the leap of faith that writing requires is through something she terms "quickwrites." By offering short, effective pieces composed by other writers, she reminds us that we too have memories, fears, joys, tragedies, dreams, information, and opinions worth exploring.

For years teachers at her workshops have listened to Linda read some short pieces and then amazed ourselves by following her direction to write quickly in response. Linda understood from the beginning that writing very fast allows us to outrun our internal censors and to let our own words untangle our thinking. She understood that the eloquence of another's words might ignite some spark of connection in readers, compelling us then to pick up the pen ourselves. Language well used, spun and woven in ways that astonish and delight, does inspire us. And somehow being asked to write for just two or three minutes seems safe for even the most recalcitrant writer. Delighted with the workshop experience, how many teachers have bombarded Linda with requests for these pieces, many composed by her eighth graders, to take back to our own classrooms? Certainly, I have been one of them.

Linda's latest gift to us is *100 Quickwrites*, her collection of student and professional pieces, including several of her own. It's a tapestry of poetry and prose gathered over the past 20 years, pieces that have nudged her kids into some extraordinary writing. Linda has been astute in her collecting. Because she knows adolescents so well, she knows what will move them: sometimes a professional piece, sometimes one by another student, sometimes one of her own. We hear the voices of beloved authors, such as Naomi Shihab Nye, Sharon Creech, and Ralph Fletcher. We hear the voices of Linda's eighth graders as they write with courage and candor about what it means to be an adolescent today. This is one of Linda's greatest strengths: she knows that "the stuff of their (sic) lives is a great cargo, and some of it heavy" (Wilbur). She makes the stuff of their lives the stuff of the writing curriculum, launching them with her quickwrites and following through with astute questions in their notebooks or in writing conferences each week. "Tell me more," she pleads, and they know she means it; she really wants to know.

Linda's students tell her, year after year, that what helps them most as writers is her habit of sharing her drafts with them. Here in *100 Quickwrites* she includes several of her own compelling pieces. Reading them, it is easy to see why so many students have been moved to set their sights high, to stretch themselves as writers, to compose poetry and prose that takes our breath away. Indeed, reading through this collection makes me want to grab my notebook and do some quick writing myself.

The quickwrite models make compelling reading. I found myself moved by Eloise Greenfield's "Mama Sewing," and equally moved by Linda's own "When She Was Fifteen;" by W. H. Auden's "Embassy," but also by Lindsay O.'s "Reverence;" by Linda Pastan's "Autumn," and also by Janet M.'s "Black River," a poem I've wanted to get my hands on for years. The models are arranged thematically, offering us the option of using them with our own particular courses of study in classrooms, although they work quite nicely as stand-alone pieces as well. Inevitably, tantalized by Linda's choices, readers will want to add to the collection our own favorite pieces, written by students, pros, or even ourselves.

Beyond helping us want to write, Linda also gives us practical and specific advice on how to teach. Worried that we are backing away from writing in our compunction to raise reading scores, she reminds us that writing will always lead to more careful reading. When we read the words of others—as we do in the pieces collected here—we are reassured that others have felt what we feel, lived through pain and doubt, survived and even thrived in this world. Finding such assurance, we are led to read more, and our reading will inevitably affect our living, which, of course, it has always been meant to do.

Habitual writing, Linda knows, will change the way we read other texts. We pay more attention to language, to pace, to leads, to the myriad ways writers discover and express meaning on the page. The quickwrite models serve as bridges, human heart to human heart. "Here is what it is like for me," we hear when we read, with the implicit question being, "What is it like for you?" Thus, we are urged to write. In our quest to come closer and closer to what it is we mean to say, we must read and reread our own words, becoming both more critical and more creative in the process.

Linda's suggestions following each quickwrite will be invaluable to teachers, whether they are beginners in the writing workshop or veterans looking for some fresh inspiration. Her careful discussion of how to help students move "beyond quickwrites" is another resource that will change the way we write and the way we teach.

Linda Rief knows that there is nothing more powerful than writing. She has high expectations of herself, of her students, and of us, her fellow teachers. The writing we do and the writing our students do must be far more than "fine;" it must startle and surprise and sparkle and shine and, ultimately, shake the world. *100 Quickwrites* offers 100 invitations that challenge us to embrace our work anew with even higher expectations. We will be in good company.

Maureen Barbieri
Steinhardt School of Education
New York University

**Reference**

Wilbur, Richard. "The Writer." In *Strings: A Gathering of Family Poems*, collected by Paul Janeczko. New York: Bradbury Press, 1984.

# Introduction

"One line of a poem, the poet said—only one line, but thank God for that one line—drops from the ceiling. . . . and you tap in the others around it with a jeweler's hammer."
—Annie Dillard, *The Writing Life*, pp.77-78

"The simple rhythm of copying someone else's words gets us into the rhythm (of writing), then you begin to feel your own words."
—William Forrester, *Finding Forrester*

". . . because, for one thing, becoming a better writer is going to help you become a better reader, and that is the real payoff."
—Anne LaMott, *Bird by Bird*

Several times a week, at the beginning of class, I put a short piece of writing on the overhead projector, read it out loud, and ask students to do a *quickwrite* in response. The results of this simple routine are astounding. Consider the following example, written by Lindsay O. after I read aloud Cynthia Rylant's picture book *When I Was Young in the Mountains*.

**Remembrance**
*For my grandmother, Clarice Smith Chapman, 1914- 1989*

I remember . . . we collected wild strawberries
And made mud pies and built
Block houses and guided
Our cart down the supermarket aisle
And picked carrots and washed
Dishes and baked cookies and cut
Paper dolls and watched chickadees
And played checkers and ate scrambled eggs and
Took our time on the stairs
And you never told me you were dying.

I wanted the chance to say goodbye.

Powerful. But not so exceptional that other students couldn't do just as well. I've found that inviting students to write off a found idea or borrowed line for just two to three minutes produces good writing—often *really* good writing. Students are always surprised by the thinking that spills out on the page. I used to be; I'm not anymore. (I now use Lindsay's poem as a model for quickwrites, to stimulate the thinking and writing of other students; it's included in this collection on page 64.)

## What Is a Quickwrite?

A *quickwrite* is a first draft response to a short piece of writing (usually no more than one page of poetry or prose, or a short picture book). To do a quickwrite, students and teacher write for two to three minutes off a found idea or borrowed line from a text, responding to something that sparks a reaction in the mind of the reader/listener. This process helps writers generate ideas and get words on paper. When I have students do a quickwrite, I specifically ask them to:

- write as quickly as they can for two to three minutes, capturing all that comes to mind in response to the work as a whole, or
- borrow a line or part of a line (one of their own choosing or a particular line that I suggest) from the work and write off (or from) that line nonstop for two to three minutes, or
- use a specific line or particular style as a model from which to write, as in the example of suggestions for Lindsay's poem, "In Remembrance: For My Grandmother, Clarice Smith Chapman."

The main purpose of doing a quickwrite is simply to get words on paper. For years I watched students staring into space, claiming they had nothing to write about. Just telling them to "write anything" didn't help; they already couldn't think of "anything." Quickwrites stimulate their thinking so that they can find words. Joel, an eighth grader, told me one day, "The quickwrites help me write down some things I didn't remember I knew. When I see them it makes me *want* to write, so I *do* write."

I can't work in a void, and neither can students. Quickwrites help them find words for their ideas in a concrete way. Once students have words on paper, I can help them develop those thoughts into effective, compelling pieces of writing. Quickwrites help all of us get out of the void.

## The Benefits of Quickwrites

Writing and teaching writing can be intimidating. It is hard work, and it takes time. Quickwrites offer an easy and manageable writing experience that helps both students and teachers find their voices and develop their confidence, as they discover that they have important things to say. This quick exercise pulls words out of the writer's mind, and I am always surprised at the precision of language, level of depth and detail, and clarity of focus I hear when a student reads a three-minute quickwrite out loud. When the models for quickwrites are compelling and carefully chosen, students are able to focus closely and write clearly.

Over the years of using these invitations to write with students in my classroom and with teachers in workshops and courses, I've discovered so many of their benefits:

*Quickwrites bring out the writer.* They:

- give students ideas and frames for their writing so that they are not working in a void.
- focus students' attention and stimulate their thinking at the beginning of a class.
- provide and capture the seeds of ideas for more expanded pieces.
- encourage writing about important ideas, chosen to make us think and feel as we learn.
- give students choices about what they write, how they write, and what works and does not work.
- help students focus on one subject in great detail by giving them examples filled with sensory detail.
- introduce students to a variety of stylistic devices and craft lessons they might try in their writing.

*Quickwrites build students' confidence.* They:

- offer surprise when students discover that they didn't realize how much they knew, or what they were thinking, until they began writing.
- build confidence when students see the quality of their writing.
- make writing accessible to all students, even those who struggle the most with words and ideas, because quickwrites are short, quick, non-threatening, and directed toward a specific task.

*Quickwrites develop fluency.* They:

- keep students writing several times a week.
- keep students writing beyond the quickwrite when they find themselves committed to a topic that matters to them.
- offer ongoing practice for writing in sensible, realistic, and meaningful ways on demand or in timed situations.

*Quickwrites bring out the reader.* They:

- teach students to become better readers as they hear, see, and craft language.
- teach students critical reading as they choose significant lines, and then draft and reconsider their ideas in the clearest ways.
- provide examples of fine, compelling writing from their peers, their teacher, and professional writers.
- introduce students to a variety of writers: poets, essayists, and fiction and nonfiction writers.

*Quickwrites help teachers grow as writers.* They

- allow us time to write for two to three minutes each class period.
- help us find ideas for writing and our voices as writers.
- clarify our understanding of the difficulty of the task we are asking students to complete, because we're doing what we've asked them to do.

# Teaching With Quickwrites

Quickwrites are a powerful teaching tool, and there are many ways to use them to spark successful writing. Although I usually only put one piece of writing on the overhead for a quickwrite, there are times when I might group two or three together and ask the students to respond to one after another, or to the group as a whole. (See "And So It Goes," "The Game," and "Dear Mr. President" as an example of a grouping.) There are endless configurations to use based on themes or issues being explored in the classroom. The writing of scientists, historical figures, mathematicians, or musicians could be used in any discipline to immerse and focus students in the thinking of these fields.

This book also includes several sketches and drawings as possibilities for stimulating ideas. Over the years I have noticed that the students who struggle the most with words find a way to start writing if they first work with their ideas visually. I give students the option to do a *quickdraw* in response to many of these pieces. The drawings may be entries into writing, or they may tell a story on their own visually, as students craft pictures in the same way they would craft words to clearly represent their message. My goal is to help students grow and become the most articulate, literate young men and women they can be in the short time that I work with them.

## Getting Started

In my teaching, I always try to remember that:

- The more I want students to know how to do something well, the more often they should do it.
- We learn to read by reading and writing.
- We learn to write by writing and reading.

Quickwrites support all three of these principles. Below are some practices I've developed around quickwrites to help students read and write successfully.

### ENGAGE STUDENTS IN WRITING

- Make a transparency out of any of the pieces of writing in this book, or others that you find are meaningful and compelling to your students.
- Let the students see the pieces by putting them on an overhead projector.
- Read the piece aloud to the students so they can hear it (practice ahead of time so that you really know the writing well).
- Ask students to try writing or drawing quickly based on any of the "Try this" ideas at the bottom of each page.
- Write or draw your own quickwrites with the students.
- If more than half of the students are still writing after 2 or 3 minutes, let them continue for another minute or two.
- Give students credit (good faith participation) for doing the quickwrites, considering this rough draft writing part of their notebook or journal writing.

ENGAGE STUDENTS IN READING

- Ask if anyone would like to read what they wrote.
- Thank any volunteers for sharing and comment specifically on what they did well.
- Read your own quickwrites to the students (ones you don't like as well as ones you like), and occasionally show them how you develop some of the ideas into more extended pieces.

EXTEND THE QUICKWRITES

- Allow the students a choice in which quickwrites remain undeveloped and which matter enough to expand or craft further into finished pieces.
- Teach the students the craft of revision as you conference with them about their writing, whether it comes from quickwrites or other sources. (See Building From the Quickwrites section at the end of the book.)
- Every few weeks, ask students to go back to their quickwrites and find one that surprised them or they want to know more about, indicating that the quickwrite could be developed into a more expanded piece. (This is easier if the quickwrites are all kept in one continuously written notebook, and it is especially helpful if students are not doing this on their own.)

EXTEND THIS COLLECTION

- Add your students' writing and your own writing to this collection.
- Add the writing of professionals that you particularly like to this collection.
- If there are particular kinds of writing you would like students to become more adept with, find models you can use as quickwrites to help them craft that kind of writing (persuasive pieces, essays, poetry, description, etc.).

# Objective of This Book

The major objective of this book is to put in the hands of teachers a collection of writing that offers compelling models for quickwrites. These models are accessible, valuable, and meaningful invitations to writers, but they are only the beginning. As teachers, we have to find ways of helping students expand and build on these initial ideas so that they will want to write and, therefore, *will* write and read. It is through the actual process of developing writing that students learn to write, and through the actual process of taking meaning from reading that students learn to read. First, though, they need to get those initial ideas onto paper. Our written and oral responses to students in conferences as they write, and through craft lessons as they draft, help them build on these nuggets of possibilities.

# Choosing Models for Quickwrites

Pieces selected for quickwrites must be complete works, not stand-alone phrases or three-word prompts. Students need to see a whole piece that is thoughtfully and carefully crafted, and they need to see something that touches them intellectually and/or emotionally. Adolescents are in the throes of immense physical, emotional, intellectual, and social growth. The pieces of writing we choose to share with them should be ones with which they can connect on many of these levels. The most valuable sources of quickwrites are short works that are:

- language rich
- strong in sensory imagery
- evocative of strong feelings
- thought-provoking
- relevant and compelling to adolescents' interests

When carefully chosen, quickwrite models also demonstrate the craft lessons we want to teach students: careful organization, compelling leads and endings, effective word choice, strong nouns and verbs, even conventions of language—or breaking the rules of conventions when done with intent. (Jay's "School Daze," found on page 25 of this collection, is a good example of breaking the rules for the conventions of language because she does it with intent, wanting the reader to be as confused as she is.)

Thoughtfully selected, quickwrite models invite students into writing in a way that encourages critical reading as they commit their voices to paper and grow as writers. I use the writing of professionals, the writing of my former students, and my own writing to stimulate thinking for quickwrites. In her journal, my student Maggie wrote, "I had never done quickwrites before, and because of the limited time given I've found myself writing things I didn't know I knew or felt. They really help me get a sense of who I am and help me come up with ideas." That is the power of a well-chosen quickwrite model.

## About the Models in This Collection

Two-thirds of the writing pieces in this book were written by the eighth-grade students I've taught over the past fifteen years in my language arts classroom. One-third of the pieces are the work of professional writers. I have used all of these pieces over and over again because they seem to stimulate the highest quality student writing year after year. I add to this collection every year, including the work of new students, the latest professional writing, and my own pieces as I continue to write. I hope that's what you will do, too. As teachers, we need to find and use the writing that works best with our own students.

I have assembled the pieces of this collection in a framework that underscores the way adolescents view themselves:

- seeing inward
- leaning outward, close to home
- stepping beyond, toward the world at large
- looking back

Each piece is followed by writing suggestions found under the heading "Try this."

The purpose of these suggestions is to help students start writing, but I always remind them to ignore my prompts if they have their own ideas.

## How to Use These Models in the Classroom

Several times a week I begin the class with one of these pieces—sometimes using them in the order in which they appear in the book, other times pulling pieces because they are related to a topic we may be studying (the Holocaust, other human rights or social justice issues, becoming a writer, relationships, and so on). I put a piece on the overhead projector so the students can see it, read it aloud to the students so they can hear it, and then ask them to write silently for two to three minutes. I may ask students to write in any of the following ways—the ways which also shape the "Try this" suggestions on each page:

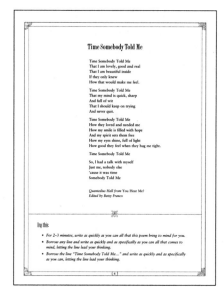

- write as quickly and as specifically as you can for two to three minutes everything that this piece of writing brings to mind for you, OR
- borrow a line and write as quickly and as specifically as you can, letting the line lead your thinking, OR
- do something specific with the writing or with a particular line from the writing, AND
- IGNORE anything I asked you to do if what I put up on the overhead already had you writing.

The whole point is to get students writing—which gets them thinking, which gets them writing, which keeps them reading and writing.

## Reader's-Writer's Notebooks

My students draft their quickwrites in the response section of their reader's-writer's notebook, so they can be collected as seeds of ideas that might be further developed. I've found that students need one place to continually collect ideas; otherwise, that writing on single sheets of paper gets tossed, buried in their lockers, or left in the classroom. Keeping their writing in one notebook or journal also allows me to respond to it regularly and easily. I read these notebooks every two weeks, affirming the thoughtfulness in their reading and writing. My response, though it may only be underlining something or jotting notes and questions, is meant to support their thinking and push them to grow as readers and writers.

My eighth graders are expected to complete three to five pages of writing in their notebooks each week. This includes their quickwrites, their responses to books or any reading they are doing at night, and the collecting of ideas for writing. Counting quickwrites toward their writing total lets students know how much I value this kind of writing and encourages them to value it, too. It encourages them to treat it as fertile ground from which further writing and thinking may spring.

## Taking Quickwrites Further

After writing, I invite students to share their work out loud to the entire class or in small groups at their tables. Sometimes many kids read what they wrote; other times, no one does. Sometimes I read my own quickwrite, while other times I might mention why I am not sharing what I wrote.

Occasionally I ask the class what they noticed about another student's writing that struck them. What did they do that made the writing so effective? What else could they do to elaborate on the idea? I also tell students that if someone reads a piece that makes them think of something else, they should jot it down before it disappears.

These quickwrites are seeds of ideas, the beginning of a piece to be worked on right away or, at the very least, captured for later use. Students have the option to continue working from or on the quickwrite, to let it just sit in their notebooks for later development, or to never work on it again.

I frequently go back to a piece of writing a second or third time to look at the questions students might have had, to look at the language of the piece, or to talk about the craft of the writing. The last section of this book is devoted to giving examples of the variety of ways in which quickwrites were used by the students to capture their ideas and/or develop them into more polished pieces of writing.

### Invitations to Writing

This book is a series of invitations to students and teachers, intended to help them find ideas for writing. It does not attempt to oversimplify a complex process. Quickwrites offer beginnings, support, connections, and encouragement in a practical, concrete, and accessible way. They help students realize that they do have something to say, and that they are capable of saying those things in a way that engages readers.

Adolescents are often uncomfortable and insecure about writing. Quickwrites are nonthreatening precisely because they are short and quick, yet focused. They provide accessible entrance into significant matters because they are chosen for their compelling topics, well-crafted language, and unique styles. When carefully selected so that students can readily relate to them, they give students models that stimulate their thinking about their own topics in concrete, specific ways. As they experiment and craft their ideas, observations, beliefs, knowledge, and opinions, students develop as critical readers and thinkers. They also develop as human beings, answering their biggest questions, such as *Who am I? Where do I fit in this world?*

A peripheral benefit of using quickwrites is that they enhance students' ability to cope with timed writing assignments on specific topics. I remind them to approach such assignments as they would a quickwrite, and to use the same process to develop, expand, revise, and edit their thinking as they take the writing to a polished draft. They are better able to face such daunting, timed tasks precisely because their quickwrite practice has made them more fluent and proficient.

Kira, a language arts teacher who is part of a course I have been teaching, literally came running to me at the beginning of the third class, breathless. "You know how I told you I hated writing and was petrified about teaching it and that I had nothing to say and no matter what you did I knew it wouldn't help me but I can't believe what I've done with these quickwrites and I was so excited I've been working with my kids all week and I've written things I didn't know I knew and they've written things they didn't know they knew and every day I can't wait to work on this writing and neither can they and I can't believe their writing can be this good."

And the writing *is* good. There is something about asking students to write quickly and for a short period of time, with good examples in front of them, that leads them to think in detailed, explicit, focused ways.

## Leading Students to Literacy

Don Graves said that "Democracies are dependent on the quality of their citizens' thinking . . . . And one of the best ways to develop solid thinkers early on is by asking children to think clearly through a written text."

In our attempts as a nation to lead our children to literacy, we have nearly abandoned writing—writing for real reasons, for real audiences. I think we have also forgotten that a person can read without writing, but he or she cannot write without reading. If we neglect writing while focusing our attention almost exclusively on reading, it is also *at the expense of reading*.

What has happened to the writing that used to flourish in classrooms? Have we forgotten, ignored, or—even worse—abandoned it? Have we dismissed long-term, real writing while focusing all of our attention on one-word answers or formulaic paragraphs to standardized, shortened passages of reading, supposedly to determine our students' critical reading skills?

Have we forgotten that *writing is thinking*? When students write, they are engaged in a recursive process of critical thinking: "Have I said clearly what I want to say? Are my thoughts well organized and my ideas clearly developed? Have I used the sharpest, tightest, most vivid language? Does my lead capture readers and give them a clear direction and focus? Does my writing make the reader think or feel or learn something?" When students are engaged in the process of writing something that matters to them, they do write and they do read, thoughtfully and thoroughly.

Our goals should be loftier than "raising reading scores." Our classrooms should be laboratories of high-level thinking where the activities stimulate our students' curiosity and imagination, where the students are the problem-solvers, the thinkers. It is through speaking, reading, *and writing* that our students become articulate, literate, confident, and thoughtful citizens of the world.

Quickwrites get students thinking.

# Professional Resources for Quickwrites

Buchwald, Emilie and Ruth Roston, eds. *This Sporting Life—Contemporary American Poems About Sport and Games*. Minneapolis, MN: Milkweed Editions, 1987.

Cisneros, Sandra. *The House on Mango Street*. New York: Random House, 1989.

Dunning, Stephen, Edward Lueders, and Hugh Smith, eds. *Reflections on a Gift of Watermelon Pickle*. New York: Scholastic, 1966.

Fletcher, Ralph. *Ordinary Things: Poems from a Walk in Early Spring*. New York: Atheneum Books, 1997.

Fletcher, Ralph. *I Am Wings: Poems About Love*. New York: Atheneum, 1994.

Franco, Betsy, ed. *You Hear Me? Poems and Writing by Teenage Boys*. Cambridge, MA: Candlewick Press, 2000.

Gaige, Amity. *We Are A Thunderstorm*. Kansas City, Missouri: Landmark Editions, 1990.

Greenberg, Jan, ed. *Heart to Heart: New Poems Inspired by Twentieth Century American Art*. New York: Harry N. Abrams, Inc, 2001.

Heard, Georgia. *Writing Toward Home*. Portsmouth, NH: Heinemann, 1995.

Janeczko, Paul. *Poetspeak: In Their Work, About Their Work*. New York: Bradbury Press, 1983.

Knudson, R.R. and May Swenson, eds. *American Sports Poems*. New York: Orchard Books, 1988.

Lowry, Lois. *The Giver*. New York: Houghton Mifflin, 1993.

Mazer, Norma Fox and Marjorie Lewis, eds. *Waltzing on Water: Poetry by Women*. New York: Dell, 1989.

McManus, Patrick F. *They Shoot Canoes, Don't They?* New York: Henry Holt and Company, 1981.

Nye, Naomi Shihab. *This Same Sky—A Collection of Poems From Around the World*. New York: Four Winds Press, 1992.

_____. *Fuel*. Rochester, NY: Boa Editions, 1998.

_____. *Sitti's Secrets*. New York: Simon & Schuster Books for Young Readers, 1994.

Nye, Naomi Shihab, ed. *What Have You Lost?* New York: Greenwillow Books, 1999.

Rylant, Cynthia. *When I Was Young in the Mountains*. New York: E. P. Dutton, 1982.

Rylant, Cynthia. Photographs by Walker Evans. *Something Permanent*. New York: Harcourt Brace, 1994.

Soto, Gary. *A Fire in My Hands*. New York: Scholastic, 1990.

Any poems, children's picture books, short essays, flash fiction, art work, and vignettes that are language rich, strong in sensory imagery, evoke strong feelings, are thought-provoking, and relevant to students' own experiences are valuable as resources for quickwrites.

# A Slice of Life

What's as confusing as last week's science lab?
Can be as sweet as sugar?
Then, sharp as a knife?
Comes quickly
But with no instructions on how to handle it?
Can take you up to the stars
Or throw you sprawling against a rock?
Just when you think you've got it figured out,
It takes an unexpected turn.
Those who have lived it
Either warn you about the dangers it brings,
Or tell you to live it to the fullest.
Perhaps you know what I am talking about.
Don't let it pass by without making a mark
Or saving a memory, because
It will only come once, and soon the opportunities,
The moments, the dreams
Will all just be a slice of your past
The piece of life that we call
Adolescence.

*Katherine T.*

## Try this:

- *Write as quickly as you can for 2–3 minutes all that this poem brings to mind for you.*
- *Borrow one of the lines and write as quickly and as specifically as you can, letting the line lead your thinking.*
- *Think about "adolescence," and describe this time period in your life. (Write as quickly and as specifically as you can.)*

Scholastic Professional Books  *100 Quickwrites* by Linda Rief

# Dandelions

I am a dreamer.

I want to fly,
but I run instead.
I see myself in the eyes of a cat,
a shadow even at night, and
I am a shadow too.

I am the dandelion nobody loves.
I am softer than peach fuzz,
not sleek like the cat,
curled on the sill
basking in bubbles of sunlight,
sunlight and feline,
bright and warm and beautiful.

Not like me.
Not like me.

Don't relate me to daffodils,
I am neither fair nor sweet.
Don't say I am a lion,
I am not brave.
Don't match my petals to the locks
of a golden-haired girl.

Please *feel* my radiance.
Brush my pollen kiss across each cheek.
Glance my way and see my
sunny smile.

Watch me stretch,
though I do not compare to the agile cat.
Watch me mourn with the earth
as raindrops slide from my foliage;
I have a heart that can be broken.
Watch me shudder
when the wind tries my strength,
and in the end I will
stand tall still.
Watch as each petal is replaced
with tufts of clouds, each clinging
to a single seed, each seed
a synonym of life itself,
floating on the breeze.
Watch these words become my wings
and then
Watch me fly.

*Graeham D.*

## Try this:

- *Write as quickly and as specifically as you can all that this poem brings to mind for you.*
- *Borrow any line from this poem and write as quickly as you can all that the line brings to mind, letting the line lead your thinking.*

Scholastic Professional Books    *100 Quickwrites* by Linda Rief

# Jen

I asked you to dance,
But you were still crying.
I gave you a rose,
But you were still depressed.
I gave you a teddy bear,
But you never received it.
I gave you a porcelain unicorn,
But you were still broken up.
I tried to be nice,
I tried to comfort you,
I tried to help you,
But none of it worked
So I cried.
And you don't know
How much it would mean to me
Just to see you,
Smile.

*Jeff B.*

## Try this:

- *For 2–3 minutes, write as quickly as you can about any experience this brings to mind for you.*
- *Borrow any line from this poem and write for 2–3 minutes, letting the line lead your thinking.*

*When I first started liking girls, about the time I was thirteen and in seventh grade, I often couldn't concentrate on my homework, which I did at the public library. I would look up, and there would be a girl I could like. G.S.*

# That Girl

The public library was saying things
In so many books,
And I, Catholic boy
In a green sweater,
Was reading the same page
A hundred times.
A girl was in my way,
Protestant or Jew.
And she was at the other end
Of the oak table,
Her hands like doves
On the encyclopedia, E–G.
England, I thought,
Germany before the war?
She'll copy from that book,
Cursive like waves
Riding to the shore,
And tomorrow walk across lawns
In a public school dress
With no guilt pulling at an ear.
And me? I'll kick
My Catholic shoes through
Leaves, stand in the
Cloakroom and eat

A friend's lunch. My work
Was never finished.
My maps were half-colored,
History a stab in the dark,
And fractions the inside
Of a pocket watch
Spilled on my desk.
I was no good. And who do I
Blame? That girl.
When she scribbled a pink
Eraser and her pony
Tails bounced like skirts,
I looked up, gazed for what
My mother and sister could not
Offer, then returned to
The same sentence: *The Nile*
*Is the longest river in the world.*
A pencil rolled from the
Table when she clicked open
Her binder. I looked up,
Gazed, looked back down:
The Nile is the longest river…

*Gary Soto from* A Fire in My Hands

## Try this:

- *For 2–3 minutes, write as quickly as you can all that Soto's words bring to mind for you.*
- *Borrow any line and write as quickly and as specifically as you can all that comes to mind, letting the line lead your thinking.*

Scholastic Professional Books     *100 Quickwrites* by Linda Rief

# Time Somebody Told Me

Time Somebody Told Me
That I am lovely, good and real
That I am beautiful inside
If they only knew
How that would make me feel.

Time Somebody Told Me
That my mind is quick, sharp
And full of wit
That I should keep on trying
And never quit.

Time Somebody Told Me
How they loved and needed me
How my smile is filled with hope
And my spirit sets them free
How my eyes shine, full of light
How good they feel when they hug me tight.

Time Somebody Told Me

So, I had a talk with myself
Just me, nobody else
'cause it was time
Somebody Told Me

*Quantedius Hall from* You Hear Me?
*Edited by Betsy Franco*

## Try this:

- *For 2–3 minutes, write as quickly as you can all that this poem brings to mind for you.*
- *Borrow any line and write as quickly and as specifically as you can all that comes to mind, letting the line lead your thinking.*
- *Borrow the line "Time Somebody Told Me . . ." and write as quickly and as specifically as you can, letting the line lead your thinking, or write about all that you wish someone did tell you.*

Scholastic Professional Books     *100 Quickwrites* by Linda Rief

# Within

There's a place within me
That sings like the sea
That dances like the ocean wind
Soft, but wild and free.

There's a place within me
That shifts like the sand
That swims like a graceful seal
Heading for the land.

There's a place within me
That sighs like the tide
That curls like a roaring wave
That the slick seals ride.

And when I walk
Upon the shore
I am not a girl
Anymore.
I slip into the sea
And
Sing
Dance
Shift
Swim
Sigh
And
Curl
Till the tide is low. . .
Once more, I'm a girl.

*Lindsay H.*

Try this:

- *For 2–3 minutes, write as quickly as you can all that this poem brings to mind for you.*
- *Borrow any line and write as quickly and as specifically as you can, letting your thinking follow that line.*

# Moon Mission: To-Do List

Grow plants in zero-G
Fix satellite
Send probe to Venus
Study sleep rhythms in space
Grow crystals in space
Space walk
Take pictures of Earth
Launch satellite
Study how ants work in space
Land in Sea of Vapors on Moon
Gather rock samples from Fra Mauro on Moon
Examine Autolycus crater on Moon
Gather moon rocks and moon dust
    from Mare Crisium on the lunar surface
Orbit Moon
Return to Earth

*Honey, when you get back, don't forget:*
A gallon of milk
A loaf of bread
Cheddar cheese

*Samuel L.*

## Try this:

- *In Samuel's style and as quickly as you can, write a "to do" list based on something you know how to do well (assemble a motor, put together a motorbike, skateboard, prepare to go hunting, get dressed to play hockey, dance, surf, etc.). End it with a list of some of the things you're made to do to show the irony in the comparison.*

- *Write out as quickly and as specifically as you can all that Samuel's words bring to mind for you.*

Scholastic Professional Books     *100 Quickwrites* by Linda Rief

# Waiting for the Splash

Last night
after you hung up
I wrote you a poem
hoping it might change your heart.

This morning I tell myself:
Get serious, man.
Someone once compared
writing a poem
and hoping it will
change the world
to dropping rose petals
down a deep well

waiting for the splash

*Ralph Fletcher from* Looking for Your Name
*Selected by Paul Janeczko*

## Try this:

- *For 2–3 minutes, write as quickly as you can all that this poem brings to mind for you.*
- *Borrow any line, and write from that line as quickly and as specifically as you can, letting the line lead your thinking.*

Scholastic Professional Books    *100 Quickwrites* by Linda Rief

# School Daze

help
i am going to be
refracted and i can't
count a present progressive
is staring me in the face with verbs crying
to be conjugated algebraic
sentences are chasing
me as i run into a mercantilist
policy a phosphorescent light appears
in front of me trying
to help me in this mass
confusion i stare at it hoping
for enlightenment
but nothing
jumps out at me so i
run head on
into a quadratic
monomial factor a voice
out of nowhere echoes around me

"You're eighth graders now!"

Then why do I feel as befuddled as ever?

*Jay S.*

## Try this:

- *For 2–3 minutes, write as quickly as you can all that this poem brings to mind for you.*
- *Borrow any line and write as quickly and as specifically as you can all that the line brings to mind.*
- *Think about all you are expected to know and do, and write as quickly as you can all those things that come to mind (home, school, music, sports, etc.).*

Scholastic Professional Books    *100 Quickwrites* by Linda Rief

# Just Me, the Ball, and the Basket

It's just me, the ball, and the basket
The crowd may roar
The players may talk trash
The officials may blow their whistles
But I don't hear them
It's a free shot
No hands waving in my face
No opponents diving and reaching at me
No twenty-four second clock ticking
No eager teammates waiting for a pass I can't make
It's just me, the ball, and the basket
I slowly raise the ball
Roll it sweetly off my fingertips
Watch its rainbow arc
Swish

*Dipta B.*

## Try this:

- *For 2–3 minutes, write as quickly as you can all that Dipta's words bring to mind for you.*
- *Borrow any line and write as quickly and as specifically as you can, letting the line lead your thinking.*

Scholastic Professional Books    *100 Quickwrites* by Linda Rief

# He Shaved His Head

He shaved his head to release his imagination.

He did it to get a tattoo on his shiny head.

He did it to lose his normality.

He did it to become a freak.

He did it because he was angry.

He did it to make people angry.

He did it for himself.

*Rene Ruiz from* You Hear Me?
*Edited by Betsy Franco*

## Try this:

- *For 2–3 minutes, write as quickly as you can all that this poem brings to mind for you.*
- *Borrow any line and write as quickly and as specifically as you can all that comes to mind, letting the line lead your thinking.*
- *Change the pronoun "he" to the first person "I," the second person "you," or the third person "she," and write about something that person did, and why, as quickly and as specifically as you can.*

Scholastic Professional Books    *100 Quickwrites* by Linda Rief

# A Day in July

Do you remember? I do.
A day in July,
we were on the beach,
our pants rolled to our calves.
The sand and salt made our ankles itch,
like lemon juice on a rash,
and the sun made my cheeks burn.
Our conversation was not heavy.
We did not talk in circles to pull us down.
Our words were light and I can't remember them,
they were lost like the bubbles on a crashing wave.
As the shadows lengthened
so did the focus on my eyes.
I knew the day would end.
My heart was in my throat,
like seaweed choking a tidal pool.
I wanted to stay on that beach with you
until the sand covered our ankles
and the moon held the tide from us.

*Janet M.*

## Try this:

- *For 2–3 minutes, write as quickly as you can about anything this poem brings to mind for you.*
- *Borrow the line "Do you remember? I do" and write as quickly as you can all that the line brings to mind.*
- *Borrow any line and write for 2–3 minutes all that the line brings to mind for you.*

Scholastic Professional Books     *100 Quickwrites* by Linda Rief

# Insanity

Hit!
Smash
Guts,
Butts,
Crush heads.
Break
Legs,
Arms,
Backs.
Men
In stacks,
All
After a ball.

*Gaston Dubois from* American Sports Poems
*Selected by R.R. Knudson & May Swenson*

## Try this:

- *For 2–3 minutes, write as quickly as you can all that this poem brings to mind.*
- *Write as quickly and as specifically as you can about any activity, trying this list technique.*
- *Write as quickly and as specifically as you can about whether you agree or disagree with the title as a description of football.*

Scholastic Professional Books    *100 Quickwrites* by Linda Rief

# Rambling Autobiography

I was born at the height of World War II just as Anne Frank was forced into Bergen-Belsen by the Nazis. I adore Brigham's vanilla ice cream in a sugar cone and dipped in chocolate jimmies. I bought my favorite jacket for a dime at the Methodist Church rummage sale. I have lied to my parents. I never read a book for pleasure until I was 38 years old. One of my students once leaned in to me in an interview and said, "My mother's having a baby; this is the one she wants." When I was 12 I set the organdy curtains in our bathroom on fire, playing with matches. My favorite place to hide was high in the maple tree in our front yard where I could spy on neighbors. I can still smell wet white sheets pulled through the ringer washer when I think of Grammy Mac. I dated Edmundo in high school because it angered my father. I fainted when I heard the sound of the zipper as the mortician closed the body bag holding my mother. I gave birth to twin sons. I once had dinner with Judy Blume. I am a teacher who writes. I want to be a writer who teaches. . . .

*Linda Rief*

## Try this:

- *For 2–3 minutes, write as quickly as you can your own "rambling autobiography."*
- *For 2–3 minutes write as quickly and as specifically as you can about any one thing this brought to mind for you.*
- *If you're stuck for starters, borrow any phrase and write off that, such as*
  - *"I was born at . . . during . . . when . . ."*
  - *". . . playing with matches . . ."*
  - *"I can still smell . . ."*

Scholastic Professional Books     *100 Quickwrites* by Linda Rief

# Liver!

*Jim B.*

Jim's drawing tells the story of his disgust for liver and his attempts to get rid of it by giving it to the dog, who will have nothing to do with it, either.

## Try this:

- *For 2–3 minutes, write as quickly and as specifically as possible all that this story brings to mind for you.*
- *Draw as quickly as possible (use stick figures, if you prefer) all that Jim's experience brings to mind for you.*

# First Television

I lost you yesterday
Captured by flickering
Images in black and white
*The first television on the block*
Your parents proudly said
*They* didn't miss
Rickety playground swings
Pumped higher and higher
Until chains slackened
Jolted and dropped us squealing
at the highest point
*They* didn't miss tag
Just the two of us chasing
Each other across the blacktop
Not even caring who was it

That particular Monday after
Your father cashed his paycheck
And brought home a TV
They cajoled you into watching
*Tell her you'll be right out*
You rolled your eyes and said
*Five minutes, just five minutes*

I waited
With a bucket of chalk, seven

Different colors for
Drawing on the sidewalk
I waited
For swings
For tag
I waited
While you made them happy
Your silenced family sitting together
Over plastic trays of TV
dinners and
a little square box that
I came to hate

My face pressed
against the
screen door
Your mom
shushed me
away with
*Don't you
have anything
better to do*
And I did
And so did
you

*Heejung K.*

## Try this:

- *For 2–3 minutes, write as quickly as you can about all that this poem brings to mind for you.*

- *Borrow any line and write as quickly and as specifically as you can all that comes to mind, letting the line lead your thinking.*

- *Think of some electronic device that has taken over your life or the life of a friend. Write as quickly and as specifically as you can all that you like, or all that you miss, as a result.*

Scholastic Professional Books    *100 Quickwrites* by Linda Rief

# Hockey

The ice is smooth, smooth, smooth.
The air bites to the center
Of warmth and flesh, and I whirl.
It begins in a game . . .
The puck swims, skims, veers,
Goes leading my vision
Beyond the chasing reach of my stick.

The air is sharp, steel-sharp.
I suck needles of breathing,
And feel the players converge.
It grows to a science . . .
We clot, break, drive,
Electrons in motion
In the magnetic pull of the puck.

The play is fast, fierce, tense.
Sticks click and snap like teeth
Of wolves on the scent of a prey.
It ends in the kill . . .
I am one of the pack in a mad,
Taut leap of desperation
In the wild, slashing drive for the goal.

*Scott Blaine from* Grab Me a Bus. . . and Other Award Winning Poems

## Try this:

- *For 2–3 minutes, write as quickly as you can all that this poem brings to mind for you.*
- *Borrow any line and write as quickly and as specifically as you can, letting the line lead your thinking.*

Scholastic Professional Books    *100 Quickwrites* by Linda Rief

# When She Was Fifteen

When she was fifteen she believed the world would be destroyed by an atomic bomb but Debbie and Pam would probably live because their fathers were rich and they had bomb shelters. She believed the most important thing in life was a date for the Junior Prom, but she'd never have one because her nose was too long, her hair was too short, her legs were too fat, and she wasn't a cheerleader. She believed David loved Paula because Paula plucked her eyebrows.

She believed she was poor because her family had a linoleum floor in the living room and only one bathroom. There was no Maytag washer or dryer at her house. Not even a Kenmore. When she was sixteen and in charge of laundry, she drove to the laundromat in Quincy, two towns away, where no one she knew could see her wash and fold her underwear in public.

Summers she worked two jobs. Days she pitched whiffle balls to five-year-olds and colored clowns from picnic benches. She made gimp bracelets and wove real Indian change purses for little kids who had no money and saved only sticks and shells and rocks. She awarded blue ribbons and red ribbons and white ribbons for jumping the highest, running the farthest, and crying the least. At night she filled Dixie cups with butterscotch sundaes floating in marshmallow. She poured strawberry frappes and chocolate milk shakes from The Fountain at Paragon Park, while the roller coaster screamed overhead with flailing arms, the gypsy lied, and the fat lady bragged about the two-headed calf. Weekends she watched Babe Ruth baseball from behind the chain link fence at the high school. David at first, Charlie at second, and Mac at catcher.

While their parents clapped and girlfriends cheered, she dated Edmundo because he was Puerto Rican and Jesse because he was black, but mostly because it angered her father....

*Linda Rief*

## Try this:

- *Start with the line, "When I was _____ (any age) I believed . . ." and write as quickly and specifically as you can about what you believed at that age.*

- *For 2–3 minutes, write everything this brings to mind for you, thinking specifically of the sights, sounds, smells, tastes, and touch associated with those happenings or people.*

- *Change the "she" to "I," "he," or "you" and write as quickly as you can all that comes to mind when you change the pronoun. Let the writing take you where it wants to go, even if it is not the truth.*

# Flaws?

There is a fat kid who is laughed at solely because he is fat. Every day he is made fun of, and every day he goes home crying. He is fat. He admits it. He tries to lose weight, but nothing works. He has zits and shaggy hair. Kids call him lard face, doughboy, and fatso. He acts like it doesn't hurt him at all. He walks by, eyes down, mouth closed, never turning, never responding to any of the taunts. On the outside, it looks like he doesn't care, but on the inside his stomach knots and his throat catches. Every time he's called a new name it slices like a paper cut. But he's become quite good at suppressing his emotions.

When this kid goes home to his trailer park house, he goes right to his computer, the gateway to his sanctuary, where he doesn't get ridiculed because of his physical appearance. If you were on the outside, looking in, you might think this kid is kind of weird—antisocial even. But he's really just a regular kid, who wants some friends, or just a friend, who might pick him for a team just once, or not groan and roll his eyes when he's assigned the seat next to him, or might ask him to his house to skateboard or play computer games . . . or might just call me by my real name for once.

*Owen A.*

## Try this:

- *For 2–3 minutes, write as quickly as you can all that this piece brings to mind for you.*
- *Think of someone you know who may have been made fun of in some way. Write as quickly and as specifically as you can all that you remember about the way this person was treated.*

Scholastic Professional Books    *100 Quickwrites* by Linda Rief

# Swinging the River

One by one they climbed out on the thickest limb,
crouched like 12-year-old Tarzans, then
jumped, whipped through needley branches,
strangling the hemp rope till their nerve broke
and they dropped thirty feet to the river.

I was second-to-last in line. Second-
to-chickenest, I guessed. I'd never done this.

Rocks and tricky currents had drowned two kids
in three years. (One was never found.)
My mother'd kill me if she knew. . . .

My turn. My shaking hands grabbed at the rope.
I didn't dare think, just jumped,
swooped down, arced up, higher, flew free,
seemed to hang in the air while the splash
reached up to swallow me, blacking out

the sun, the feathery pine trees,
the blonde girl on the bank. . .
. . . who'd said hi the day before,
who was here with her aunt for two short weeks.

I sank like an anvil. Colder and colder.
I quietly gave up hope. Then my feet
touched a dead kid. Slime-hands
clutched at me. I kicked wildly
into sickening ooze, broke free, went shooting up

through millions of bubbles, rocketing out
into the blonde girl's smile.

*Charles Harper Webb from* Preposterous
*Selected by Paul Janeczko*

## Try this:

- *For 2–3 minutes, write as quickly as you can all that this poem brings to mind for you.*
- *Borrow any line and write as quickly and as specifically as you can, letting the line lead your thinking.*

Scholastic Professional Books    *100 Quickwrites* by Linda Rief

# When I Was Young at the Ocean

*With thanks to Cynthia Rylant for* When I Was Young in the Mountains

*When I was young at the ocean*, I sat at the edge of the wooden pier and dangled my toes in the water. Like tiny rowboats my toes skimmed the rolling waves, ever alert for sharks. Sometimes I sat cross-legged in shorts and tee-shirt, a bamboo fishing pole stretched to catch mackerel. No one ever told me to bait the hook.

When I was young at the ocean, I cracked open mussels and periwinkles and clams, and ran my fingers across their gushy insides. I squished seaweed nodules between my forefinger and thumb, anxious for the pop and spray from the moist insides.

When I was young at the ocean, I burned my shoulders and smelled of Noxzema through the entire month of July. I drank in the aroma of hip roses, salt water, and seaweed. At low tide I played croquet with the Queen of Hearts, flew to the moon in a hammock, and fed my dolls deviled ham sandwiches in the shade of the screened house.

As the tide came in, water lapped at the rocky shore. The skin of my feet toughened as I paced those rounded stones, my eyes searching for skippers. *When I was young, I never wished to climb the mountains, or live in the city, or camp in the forest. The ocean was enough. It still is.*

*Linda Rief*

## Try this:

- *Think of a place that you love (mountains, sitting in an oak tree, a fort, lake, etc.) and write as quickly as you can about all that you see, smell, touch, hear, taste, and do there.*
- *Borrow Rylant's line "When I was young in the . . . (or at the . . .)" and write as quickly as you can all that comes to mind about that place.*

Scholastic Professional Books    *100 Quickwrites* by Linda Rief

# Ringside

It all started when a new teacher held up
this picture and asked, "What's going on here?"
Everybody said how pretty the yellow house
was, the pink blossoms, the blue sky.
I said, "It's creepy. The sidewalk leads
right to the cellar." The teacher beamed
and the McKenzie brothers made fists.

I ran for the library faster than usual.
I asked Miss Wilson for more by the same guy.
She could only find one—*Stag at Sharkey's*.

I looked at that painting every day. I looked
at every inch. I looked until I was at ringside,
until I was the fighter in the modest black
trunks.

When Bobby McKenzie finally caught me
and bloodied my nose, I put my head against
his and hit him with my right and to my surprise
he winced and went down.

"Stag at Sharkey's," I bellowed. He looked
at me like I was crazy, scrambled to his feet,
and ran.

*Ron Koertge from* Heart to Heart
*Edited by Jan Greenberg*

## Try this:

- *Think about all this poem brings to mind for you and write your own "Stag at Sharkey's" as specifically and as quickly as you can.*

- *Borrow the line "It all started when . . ." and write as quickly as you can for 2–3 minutes.*

- *Borrow any line from the poem and write as quickly as you can, in any direction it takes you, for 2–3 minutes.*

Scholastic Professional Books    *100 Quickwrites* by Linda Rief

# Syncros Hinged Mountain Head Stem

*Congratulations! You've just purchased the highest quality Aheadset handlebar stem in the world. Your new Syncros Stem features the original recessed split cotter clamp mechanism. It is easy to adjust and has no protruding bolts that might end up shredding your private parts. Unique to our stem is the Syncros Wedge Lock TM, designed to replace the "star fangled nut" on Ahead Sets. Our Wedge Lock reinforces the fork steerer for a more solid headset adjustment that won't vibrate loose. Handmade from 6061 T6 hard drawn, solution heat-treated aircraft aluminum, our stem can absorb more than three times the shock of prehistoric Cro-moly stems without sacrificing precision steering. The massive, differentially tapered, extension tube and twin bolt, monocoque, handlebar clamp are designed for high lateral rigidity giving you the fingertip control you need to snake through heavily treed or rocky terrain. . . .*

These are the words I first read when I tore open the small box like a hyperactive dog with rabies. At first I just sat there and looked at the stem for awhile, until my brother finally asked if I was going to put it on my bike. I managed to mumble a few words before I trotted down to my room and started to disassemble my stock stem from the steerer tube and handlebar.

Installation was about the easiest thing I have ever done. Just line it up and tighten the Wedge Lock, which is a cylinder inside the stem about 1" long and about 1/2" wide with a large groove in it so that the steerer tube fits in it when tightened with a cotter bolt running through that horizontally. When tightened there are no bolts sticking out that you might shred your knees on, or in a worst case scenario, your private parts. Once that is done, undo the bolts on the hinge, open it up, and align your handlebar and tighten it down. After that, screw on the headset cap that comes with the stem.

My old stem was −5 degrees and this one had a +15 degree rise so it took some getting used to. Once out on the trail I eventually began to like the rise better. During some hard core rides, I figured I would see how, or how not, flexible the stem was. It turned out that this is probably one of the most rigid stems I've ridden. Due to the hinge I thought that after a lot of riding the hinge would give some and my handlebar would have some wobble in it, but there was none at all. Oh, how popular I was when I went riding with my school team.

*Trapper S.*

## Try this:

- *For 2–3 minutes, write as quickly as you can all that this description brings to mind for you.*
- *Trapper is really knowledgeable about mountain bikes. Write as quickly and as specifically as you can about something you do and know well.*

Scholastic Professional Books    *100 Quickwrites* by Linda Rief

# Owl Pellets

A month ago
in biology lab
you sat close to me
knee touching mine
your sweet smell
almost drowning out
the formaldehyde stink
which crinkled up
your nose
while I dissected
our fetal pig.

Now I take apart
this owl pellet
small bag that holds
skin and hair and bones
little skeletons
what the owl ate

but couldn't digest
and coughed back up.

You sit with Jon Fox
ignore me completely
laugh at his dumb jokes
let your head fall onto
his bony shoulder
while I attempt
to piece together
with trembling hands
the tiny bones
of a baby snake.

Certain things
are just about
impossible
to swallow.

*Ralph Fletcher from* I Am Wings

## Try this:

- *For 2–3 minutes, write as quickly as you can all that this poem brings to mind for you.*
- *Borrow Fletcher's words, "Certain things are just about impossible to swallow. . ." and write as quickly and as specifically as you can all that line brings to mind.*
- *Borrow any line from this poem and write as quickly as you can all that comes to mind.*

Scholastic Professional Books      *100 Quickwrites* by Linda Rief

# I need to find a place

I need to find a place
Where friendship never burns out.

I need to find a place
Where I can scream and shout.

I need to find a place
Where love is forever
Where you don't give up—never!

I need to find a place
That is comforting and calm.
A place—where nothing goes wrong.

*Emily G.*

## Try this:

- *For 2–3 minutes, write as quickly as you can all that comes to mind, when you read this poem.*
- *Borrow any line and write as quickly and as specifically as you can, letting the line lead your thinking.*

Scholastic Professional Books     *100 Quickwrites* by Linda Rief

# Edge of Life

If I had a life I could live
Then I'd travel to places unknown.
With you in my heart, I'd begin at the start
And never would I be alone.

A voice in the evening is calling
It tears at my soul like a fire.
Yet I cannot forget the time when we met
And the burning of that newfound desire.

I love you, I say in the darkness
I feel that I must hold you near.
Yet you slip through my grasp, like the hours
gone past
And that voice is still all I can hear.

It tells me to travel to mountains
And to places where valleys are green.
Yet it's hard to let go of the things that I
know
And the love and the hardship I've seen.

If I had a dream I could give you
I would wrap it in velvet and pearls
And send it away on the rush of the wind
That would carry it over the world.

The night holds on to me tightly
And she won't let me out in the cold.
I've reaped what I've sown, and I've called
this place home
Still I'm searching for something to hold.

If I had a life I could live
Then I'd travel to places unknown.
With you in my heart, I'd begin at the start
And never would I be alone.

With tears in my eyes I speak to you
Through the blindness of good and of bad
Please forget what I've said, for the feelings
are dead.
You're the best friend that I've ever had.

And if I had a dream I could give you
I'd wrap you in velvet and pearls
And send it away on the rush of the wind
That would carry it over the world.

I still have a life I'm not living.
I must get to those places unknown.
With you in my heart, I will end where I start
And never will I be alone.

*Abigail Lynne Becker from* A Box of Rain
*(Song written for guitar accompaniment.)*

## Try this:

- *For 2–3 minutes, write as quickly as you can all that this poem brings to mind for you.*
- *Borrow any line and write as quickly and as specifically as you can, letting the line lead your thinking.*

Scholastic Professional Books     *100 Quickwrites* by Linda Rief

# Hibiscus

Evergreen branches
sway in the pry of the
docile breeze;
clouds,
carded wool,
dance on tiptoe across the sky.

Hibiscus flowerets
fold drowsily in
buds,
raspberry pink
amidst fern-like leaves,
curled delicately,
tiny and pale,
a sleeping baby's fingers.

And somewhere in this world
a baby sleeps,
someone is falling in love,
the pussywillows bloom,
an oyster shell reveals two pearls, and
you finally believe in yourself.

*Graeham D.*

## Try this:

- *For 2–3 minutes, write as quickly as you can all that this piece brings to mind for you.*
- *Borrow any line from the text, and write off that line as quickly and as specifically as you can, letting the line lead your thinking.*

Scholastic Professional Books    *100 Quickwrites* by Linda Rief

Emily P.

## Petrified gray face

Petrified gray face
Tell us your scary story
We dare to listen.

*Erica S.*

Stare them down, brave woman
With your empty hollow eyes
It will be done soon.

*Kira G.*

Frowning in the dark
Alone, not to be disturbed
Always by yourself.

*Jordan S.*

## Try this:

- *Look at the face Emily drew in response to an art exhibit by Alan Magee—and the haiku verses written here. Write as quickly and as specifically as you can (in prose or in verse) all that comes to mind for you.*

- *Look at the face Emily drew and write your own haiku based on what you see or think.*

- *Borrow any line from one of the haiku verses and, letting the line lead your thinking, write as quickly and as specifically as you can.*

Scholastic Professional Books     *100 Quickwrites* by Linda Rief

# My mother always wanted

a graceful daughter
so she enrolled me in
Mme. DuPont's
School of Ballet
for Young Mademoiselles.
I practiced for
a month until my toes
bled and my legs throbbed.
I quit, gracefully.

Then my mother hired
a tutor, so that I
could *excel* in my studies.
I didn't like this
woman and eventually
told her "You have a
bad attitude."
She never came back.

I grinned, excellently.

My mother then convinced
me to take violin lessons. At first
I loved the responsibility
and the sophistication needed to play
such a sleek instrument,
which cost my parents
a hefty sum. But the
sticky rosin, the
laborious practicing, and
the heavy case thudding
against my leg
became tiresome.
I packed the violin away, quietly.

When will she learn?

*Heejung K.*

## Try this:

- *For 2–3 minutes, write as quickly as you can all that this poem brings to mind for you.*
- *Borrow any line and write as quickly and as specifically as you can, letting the line lead your thinking.*

Scholastic Professional Books     *100 Quickwrites* by Linda Rief

# The Hole in My Suit

*Danielle M.*

---

Danielle used sketches to show a summer day, one she spent doing all kinds of sports and activities with lots of friends and her grandmother—none of whom ever told her about the hole (exaggerated in her drawing!) in her bathing suit.

## Try this:

- *In words, describe as quickly and as specifically as you can an embarrassing event or moment that came to mind as a result of seeing Danielle's embarrassing discovery.*

- *Describe the same event using specific pictures or symbols to show all that happened in just a few frames. Pick the funniest, most embarrassing moments to highlight, but be sure to show enough so that someone else could tell your story without your help.*

Scholastic Professional Books    *100 Quickwrites* by Linda Rief

# Nail Biting

Nail biting is a disease. It's contagious. My sister caught it from me. I've tried to find a cure. The special nail polish, the kind that tastes like rotten eggs, lasts for a week. But I'd chew it off. Mom used to bribe me. But even as a kid, candy and pennies didn't tempt me.

Letting my nails grow so that I can make them look nice doesn't work either. It just takes too much time. Some people spend hours buffing, polishing, and painting. Three coats of polish take a long time to dry. People paint patterns, like intricate rosebuds, family portraits, yachts, or even love messages. The designs are so tiny that it becomes a painstaking and lengthy job.

The nail polish also has to match your outfit, or clash. For every new outfit you must have a new color. Remember, each bottle of nail polish costs around $5. Queen Blue to go with your soccer uniform. Jade to go with your forest green sweater. Crimson Red to go with your red lipstick.

Biting my nails takes a lot less time, energy, and money.

However, nail biting is an ugly disease. It leaves scars. Your cuticles become ripped and your nails become rough. Sometimes it even hurts if you bite them too short. I've bitten my nails until my fingers bleed.

Why do I bite my nails? Is there some magnetic attraction between my nails and my teeth? Craving for enamel? Vitamin deficiency?

Tests make me bite them, especially the tests that teachers keep putting off. Scary movies make me bite my nails. Games and sports are the worst. Any sport in which I'm not constantly in action means my nails are under attack. Books are great to read, but they are my nails' worst enemy. A suspenseful book, such as Agatha Christie's *Death on the Nile*, devastates my nails. Somebody has to find a cure.

Some people grow out of their nail biting. But it has stuck with me, even though my friends and family bug me about it. They say my nails are disgusting and I have to stop biting them. It doesn't work.

What's the solution? Band-Aids don't work. Plastic nails keep falling off. I think I'll get braces; people who have them say they get in the way, so they quit chewing their nails. I'm sure I'll be able to maneuver my nails around the braces on my teeth.

Actually though, I am getting worried. I'm almost in high school, and chewing my nails doesn't seem like a very sophisticated thing to do. That might stop me.

*Emma T.*

## Try this:

- *For 2–3 minutes, write as quickly as you can all that this piece brings to mind for you.*
- *Write as quickly and as specifically as you can about a bad habit you or someone you know can't seem to break.*

Scholastic Professional Books    *100 Quickwrites* by Linda Rief

# Mama Sewing

I don't know why Mama ever sewed for me. She sewed for other people, made beautiful dresses and suits and blouses, and got paid for doing it. But I don't know why she sewed for me. I was so mean.

It was all right in the days when she had to make my dresses a little longer in the front than in the back to make up for the way I stood, with my legs pushed back and my stomach stuck out. I was little then, and I trusted Mama. But when I got older, I worried.

Mama would turn the dress on the wrong side and slide it over my head, being careful not to let the pins stick me. She'd kneel on the floor with her pin cushion, fitting the dress on me, and I'd look down at that dress, at that lopsided, raw-edged, half-basted, half-pinned thing—and know that it was never going to look like anything. So I'd pout while Mama frowned and sighed and kept on pinning.

Sometimes she would sew all night, and in the morning I'd have a perfectly beautiful dress, just right for the school program or the party. I'd put it on, and I'd be so ashamed of the way I acted. I'd be too ashamed to say I was sorry.

But Mama knew.

*Eloise Greenfield and Lessie Jones Little*
*from* Childtimes: A Three-Generation Memoir

## Try this:

- *For 2–3 minutes, write as quickly as you can all that this memory brings to mind for you.*
- *Think of a time you were ungrateful toward someone who did something for you and describe that time in as much detail as you can for 2–3 minutes.*
- *Borrow the line "I don't know why . . .," adding any person and event to the sentence, and write for 2–3 minutes about all that happened.*

Scholastic Professional Books     *100 Quickwrites* by Linda Rief

# Audition

Stage-light alone
Burns life into anxious hollows
I will always own.
Knowingly enveloped in merciless watching
I am who I'm meant to be.
The meddler Time accepts defeat;
I can listen to echoes.
Streaming pulses of my pride and gift
Fly on waving unbroken wings
Landing to await judgement from harsh ears.
Intense devotion blazes alive inside me,
Swelling all the way up to my eyes.
It mingles with the final notes of my brave song
And triumphs through my hidden chaos.
The world has left me for a moment
With only my love for pretending
And the fulfilling burning intensity of a
Stage-light alone.

*Emily A.*

## Try this:

- *For 2–3 minutes, write as quickly and as specifically as you can all that this poem brings to mind for you.*

- *Borrow any line and write as quickly and as specifically as you can, letting the line lead your thinking.*

- *Think of a time you've been in the "spotlight" for any reason and write as quickly and as specifically as you can all that you thought and felt in the experience.*

Scholastic Professional Books    *100 Quickwrites* by Linda Rief

# To a Daughter Leaving Home

When I taught you
at eight to ride
a bicycle, loping along
beside you
as you wobbled away
on two round wheels,
my own mouth rounding
in surprise when you pulled
ahead down the curved
path of the park,
I kept waiting
for the thud
of your crash as I
sprinted to catch up,
while you grew
smaller, more breakable
with distance,
pumping, pumping
for your life, screaming
with laughter,
the hair flapping
behind you like a
handkerchief waving
goodbye.

*Linda Pastan from* Carnival Evening:
New and Selected Poems, 1968-1998

## Try this:

- *For 2–3 minutes, write as quickly as you can all that this poem brings to mind for you.*
- *Borrow any line and write as quickly and as specifically as you can, letting the line lead your thinking.*
- *Borrow the line "When I taught you . . ." or change the line to "When you taught me . . ." and write as quickly and as specifically as you can all that comes to mind.*

Scholastic Professional Books    *100 Quickwrites* by Linda Rief

# On Being Asked to Select
# the Most Memorable Day in My Life

Five-thousand-thirty-seven. That's how many days I have to choose from. How could I just pick one that's my most memorable?

The day I turned ten? The day my brother, dad, and I hiked Mt. Washington? The day I rode my first horse? The day I won my first blue ribbon with him? The day I first met my youngest brother? The day I won the Young Naturalist Award? The day I finally learned how to do a parallel turn in skiing? The day I first held my boxer puppy?

But I don't remember the days. I remember the moments. I don't remember the day I turned ten. I remember eleven pink candles on a chocolate cake, one for good luck. I don't remember the day I won my first blue ribbon with my horse. I just remember the feel of that last jump, how the world seemed to hold still and we were in the air for too long not to be flying. I remember the buttercups I had wound into his braided mane. I don't remember the day I finally learned how to parallel ski. I just remember the second when everything came together and I was suddenly gliding down over the bright, white snow that was making rainbows dance off my skis.

I don't remember whole days. Just moments, that I can't give a date or a time. When I was little I tried to capture the brilliant light of stained glass windows in my hands and carry it home. Moments are like that; I can't hold them but I still remember them.

*Rebecca K.*

## Try this:

- *For 2–3 minutes, write as quickly as you can all that Rebecca's words bring to mind for you.*
- *Think of one or several of your most memorable moments. Quickly and specifically, describe the moments that linger with you.*

Scholastic Professional Books    *100 Quickwrites* by Linda Rief

# Without its stones a stream would lose its song

What do you do
when they try to roll you out flat
like pie dough
on a rolling pin,
like they have to make it perfect
and get all the bumps out?
(Don't flatten out.)
What do you do
when they try to strain you
like orange pulp
through a juicer,
like all they want are the perfect, clear parts?
(Clog up the strainer.)
What do you do
when they try to cut you into shapes

like cookies,
and they're the stencil or the cookie cutter,
like you have to be a certain way?
(Stick to the cutter.)
What do you do
when they try to slice you up into little pieces
like a loaf of bread or something?
(Don't give under the knife.)
So what do you do
when they give up
and don't try to do anything
anymore?

Sing.

*Caitlin F.*

## Try this:

- *For 2–3 minutes, write as quickly as you can all that Caitlin's words bring to mind for you.*

- *Borrow any line from the poem, and write as quickly and as specifically as you can, letting the line lead your thinking.*

- *Start with the line "What do you do when . . ." and write as quickly and specifically as you can, letting the line lead your thinking.*

Scholastic Professional Books      *100 Quickwrites* by Linda Rief

# She Thinks I Don't Know

I hug my knees to my chest and press my back against the cold metal of my bed. I hear the squeak of her door closing, her feet heavy on the floor. I hear the faint thumps of things being moved, and suddenly, the clink of a bottle to glass pierces the room, too shrill and high for my ears. Too painful for me. Mom's drinking. Again.

She thinks she's so clever, the way she hides it under things in her room. But I find it. She thinks she's so good, the way she covers her breath with cinnamon candies and mints. But I smell it—the hot, putrid stink of wine that makes me want to cry, to puke, to faint, to yell all at the same time. I hate that smell.

What is going through her mind as she savors her forbidden drink? Does she think of the pain it brings to David, and Dad, and me to see her like this? Does she think of how embarrassed I am to have friends over, especially when it's really bad?

She thinks I don't know. I wish I didn't.

*Alison A.*

## Try this:

- *For 2–3 minutes, write as quickly as you can all that this piece brings to mind for you.*
- *Borrow any line and write as quickly and as specifically as possible all that comes to mind, letting the line lead your thinking.*
- *Borrow any line but change any of the pronouns to the third-person "he," the first-person "I," or second-person "you," and let this new line lead your thinking (for example: "You think you're so clever . . .").*

Scholastic Professional Books    *100 Quickwrites* by Linda Rief

# The Sadness Tree

It's a small rope
And it hangs down from
A tree beyond the field.

I tied it there many years ago.
I swung there when I was sad
And now that I have grown and moved away,
I remember.

It broke once,
So I repaired it with old shoelaces
And my Dad's strong tape.

But now, when I'm sad,
Where will I go?

It's hard to live in a circular motion
That revolves around mediocrity.
Will I fall when everything is going wrong?
I suppose I could tie
Another rope to another tree . . .

But it will never be the same.

*Abigail Lynne Becker from* A Box of Rain

## Try this:

- *For 2–3 minutes, write as quickly as you can all that this poem brings to mind for you.*
- *Borrow any line and write as quickly and as specifically as you can, letting the line lead your thinking.*
- *Think about your own version of a "sadness tree," and write as quickly and as specifically as you can about where you go or used to go.*

Scholastic Professional Books     *100 Quickwrites* by Linda Rief

# Franz Dominquez

I don't know whose fault it is.
There's enough blame to go around.
I always order a hamburger in a restaurant.
I can't read the menu.
I memorize the number of stops on the train.
I can't read the signs.
I know TV cartoons by heart.
*TV Guide* is much too hard for me.
I think I could learn to read if someone sat with me.
But teachers don't seem to have the time.
Words fly right by me.
Sometimes, when no one's around, I punch the wall.
I'm frightened by my own anger.

*Mel Glenn from* Class Dismissed!

## Try this:

- *For 2–3 minutes, write as quickly as you can all that this poem brings to mind for you.*
- *Borrow any line and write as quickly and as specifically as you can, letting the line lead your thinking.*

Scholastic Professional Books    *100 Quickwrites* by Linda Rief

# Where I Live

You will come into an antique town
whose houses move apart
as if you'd interrupted
a private discussion. This is the place
you must pass through to get there.
Imagining lives tucked in
like china plates, continue driving.
Beyond the landscaped streets,
beyond the last colonial gas station
and unsolved by zoning,
is a road. It will take you
to old farmhouses and trees
with car-tire swings.
Signs will announce hairdressing
and night crawlers.
The timothy grass will run beside you
all the way to where I live.

*Wesley McNair from* Wherever Home Begins
*Selected by Paul Janeczko*

## Try this:

- *For 2–3 minutes, write as quickly as you can all that this poem brings to mind for you.*
- *Borrow any line and write as quickly and as specifically as you can all that comes to mind, letting the line lead your thinking.*
- *Describe as quickly and as specifically as you can what someone would see if he or she were following directions to where you live.*

Scholastic Professional Books     *100 Quickwrites* by Linda Rief

# And I'm Not Ready

My mother talks to me
As she's cooking
The roast she prepares
Doesn't have its familiar smell
Outside the snow is cold
Each flake falling like a lonely leaf
Mom drops her head in her hands
And I can see her reflection
Off the glassy finish of the table
She looks
Sad
Tired
She says I will have to be more mature
To act older
Me?
The little girl who wears ponytails in her hair?
The little girl who somersaults down the hall?
The little girl who plays with dolls?
To act older?
No matter how much I try to prevent
Her leaving
It's going to happen anyway

And it does

She leaves

It's like an intense wind
Fiercely blowing
Pushing at me
Pushing the child right out of me

And I'm not ready

*Stacey S.*

## Try this:

- *For 2–3 minutes, write as quickly as you can all that this poem brings to mind for you.*
- *Borrow any line and write as quickly and as specifically as you can, letting the line lead your thinking.*
- *Borrow the line "No matter how much I try to . . ." and write as specifically and as quickly as you can, letting the line lead your thinking.*

( 57 )

# Split Second

My friend had just bought a BB gun, so we decided to go on a little hunting trip. I thought it would be fun because I love adventure.

We decided to hunt in the woods behind my house. We chose a seat behind the massive root system of a fallen pine tree as our lookout. It was well into fall and most of the trees had lost their colorful foliage and stood shivering in the cool autumn breeze. We sat and waited for awhile, but we neither heard nor saw anything. A few minutes later a flock of southbound geese flew over. We each took a few shots, but didn't hit anything.

A few minutes later we heard a chirp on the tree behind us. We whipped around to see a small bird climbing the back, already halfway up the tree. My friend brought his gun to his shoulder and fired. A split second later the bird fell to the ground. It wasn't dead, but it was suffering as it flinched and shook spasmodically.

Since I had the most powerful gun, I had to kill it. I raised my gun, and shot it. I thought hunting would be fun, but when I killed that bird, it made me feel sick.

*Steve L.*

Try this:

- *For 2–3 minutes, write as quickly as you can all that this experience brings to mind for you.*
- *Borrow a line, or a part of a line ("My friend had a . . .," "We decided to . . .," etc.) and write as quickly and as specifically as you can, letting the line lead your thinking.*

Scholastic Professional Books    *100 Quickwrites* by Linda Rief

# Socrates

I struggled. I fumed. I cut, basted, sewed, stretched, pulled . . . tried every possible way to make it look right. I glued, poked, pinched, and stuffed. It was done. At last. What was it?

It was supposed to be a platypus. Yes, one of those strange, yet pleasing, mammals from Australia. This one was fuzzy blue with black velveteen feet and bill. But, it didn't look like it was supposed to look. On the pattern's envelope was a picture of an adorable, furry, rotund, plump platypus—uniform and symmetrical. My creation was very different. One eye was smaller than the other. The bill was crooked. It wasn't stuffed enough so it was very mushy. The feet were all different shapes and sizes: some with toes, some without, one long and thin, another short and fat. And the body seams curved like meandering roads.

I was aghast. My first sewing project was a total failure. I was ashamed to show my classmates, who were busy stitching their puffy hamburgers, smiley faces, and soccer balls.

"I'm done," I announced, to no one in particular. Everyone looked up and crowded around. I was embarrassed as I looked at my deformed platypus, yet the others thought it was great.

"Oh, it's so cute!" exclaimed Gina.

"Hey! That guy's pretty awesome!" cried Greg.

Sonya grabbed him and planted a kiss on his sleek bill. "I love him!" she said.

"Gosh," I thought out loud, "I guess he's not that bad after all."

Later, I scrutinized my platypus in the privacy of my bedroom. I plopped him down on a pillow as I sat on my bed and inspected him. I decided his irregularities added character. "Socrates, I think you're pretty neat after all," I told him.

*Ming-Hui F.*

---

## Try this:

- *As specifically as you can, write for 2–3 minutes all that Ming-Hui's experience brings to mind for you.*

- *Borrow one of the lines, such as, "It was supposed to be a . . .," and write as quickly as you can, letting the line lead your thinking.*

- *Think of a time when something you tried to do went wrong, and write as quickly and as specifically as you can all that happened.*

Scholastic Professional Books    *100 Quickwrites* by Linda Rief

# Days at the Farmhouse

When I was a little girl living in my family's farmhouse, we had many pets. The goats and sheep stayed in the barn, while the cats and dogs lived in the house. I used to walk to the barn down the long, curvy dirt driveway in the back of our house. I held onto my mother's soft, strong hand, with my dad and my sisters trailing behind as we walked. I inhaled the warm, spring air as we reached the field where the goats and sheep were grazing.

My younger sister squealed whenever a sheep licked her salty fingers. My mom, still holding my hand, helped me pick a bouquet of dandelions and clovers. My dad carried handfuls of hay as he walked through the bright green grass toward the goats. With his big, dark fingers, he fed their hungry mouths. He used to pick up my small body, up and over the pointy fence to pet the sheep.

Spring in the field changed to popsicles dripping down my salty fingers in the sweltering heat of the summer sun. With my yellow jump rope I skipped down to the barn and whipped rocks into the humid air. I used to stop at the well to fill a bucket of water for the hot, sweaty animals. As I was pouring the icy, cool water into their dirty dishes, they lapped it up with their rough tongues.

In September the fields turned to piles of newly raked red and yellow leaves. With pieces of grass and leaves stuck in our hair from jumping in piles of leaves, my sister and I tumbled our way down to the barn. We both stepped up onto the wooden stools to look into the pen of goats. As my outstretched hand smoothed their rough curls, I noticed that their wool coats were quickly growing back.

Now it is December. Leaves give way to white, frosty windows. I walk down the short, not so curvy dirt driveway, alone. My dull brown boots, covered in muddy slush are buried under snow. When I reach the barn my pink fingers wrap slowly around the metal handle and I step into the barn. It doesn't smell like hay anymore and there is no sound except my breath escaping into the cold air. It numbs my nose. Everything is gone. The goats and sheep have been given away, the family has left, and I am too old to be picked up.

Divorce will do that to a family.

*Kirsten J.*

## Try this:

- *For 2–3 minutes, write all that Kirsten's memory brings to mind for you.*

- *Choose any segment of time (seasons, weeks, minutes, etc.) and think of something that changed during that time. Write as quickly and specifically as you can all that you remember about the change.*

- *For 2–3 minutes, describe through your writing how something disappointed, saddened, or changed you.*

Scholastic Professional Books    *100 Quickwrites* by Linda Rief

# If Only

If only I could shelter you
From the pain,
The longing.
If only I could dry your eyes
And let you cry no more.

I'd wrap you tight
Inside my heart.
I'd listen on those darkening nights
When nothing sounds
But silence.
Creeping in through
The cracks in your soul—

Spilling out in a distorted jumble
Leaving you with nothing
But an overwhelming emptiness.

If only I could shelter you,
Keep you from the pain.

If only I could make the moment last.
I'd hold on tight
Inside my heart
Where pain would never
Find you.

Yet, the time has come
And gone again
And still, I am but a friend.

If I thought it would help,
I'd lie for you,
Take your pain, make it my own.
If I thought it would help,
I'd cry for you.

I'd take your strength, wind it tight
And spin it out into the world.

Everyone would know
You cannot be broken.

*Abigail Lynne Becker from* A Box of Rain

---

## Try this:

- *For 2–3 minutes, write as quickly as you can all that this poem and/or drawing brings to mind for you.*
- *Borrow any line and write as quickly and as specifically as you can, letting the line lead your thinking.*

Scholastic Professional Books    *100 Quickwrites* by Linda Rief

# Norman Moskowitz

My grandfather's picture sits on my desk
While I do my homework.
My father spent money on me.
My grandfather spent time.
As I struggle with trig and other responsibilities
I remember how my grandfather would
Take me for walks in the park,
Explain how a screwball was thrown,
Encourage me to think well of myself.
I really don't want to wrestle with world history,
The gross national product and Nathaniel Hawthorne.
I just want to go to the park with you again, Grandpa.

*Mel Glenn from* Class Dismissed!

## Try this:

- *For 2–3 minutes, write as quickly as you can about all that this poem brings to mind for you.*

- *Borrow any line and write as quickly and specifically as you can, letting the line lead your thinking.*

- *Whose picture sits on your desk? Write as quickly and as specifically as you can all that the picture brings to mind for you.*

Scholastic Professional Books     *100 Quickwrites* by Linda Rief

# On Visiting My Great-Aunt
# Who Lived in a Three-Decker in Dorchester

I hated Aunt Judy's polyester dresses, thick stockings, crooked seams, square-heeled shoes, tightly frizzed permed hair, coke-bottle glasses, and wet smooches that slid down my cheek. So I turned her cream to butter, flushed her chain toilet over and over, and climbed onto her brocade sofa with dirty shoes, she yelling "No, no, Linda! Not on Great-Gramma's sofa!" So I pushed off hard with my foot and climbed onto the stool of the player piano, locked my fingers underneath the keys, slid to the edge 'til my toes reached the pedal and pumped hard until the paper songs flapped and slapped endlessly on the roll.

Sent outside "to play" I pulled all the strawberry plants from her backyard and handed her the nosegay of white petals hoping she'd yell at me, but she took them in hand like an old maid bride with a thank you and a warm smile for my father so that I couldn't back away from her musty, mothball smell that choked my air or the rhinestone broach that pricked my skin when she pulled me close and pinched my arms together so tight that I folded like an accordion and whispered, so close my face was showered with her spit, and so close my father couldn't hear, "Be good, for goodness sake, or I'll slap your hiney when your father isn't looking!"

*Linda Rief*

## Try this:

- *For 2–3 minutes, write as quickly as you can all that this piece brings to mind for you.*
- *Think of someone you really dislike and/or have been mean to, or of a person you really like and have been nice to. With this person in mind, write as quickly and as specifically as you can how you have treated this person.*
- *Think of someone who has been mean to you and describe as quickly and as specifically as you can how you've been treated by this person.*
- *Change any of the writing you did to first-person "I," second-person "you," or third-person "he/she" and notice how it changes your writing.*

( 63 )

# Remembrance

*For my grandmother*
*Clarice Smith Chapman, 1914–1989*

I remember . . . we collected wild strawberries
And made mud pies and built
Block houses and guided
Our cart down the supermarket aisle
And picked carrots and washed
Dishes and baked cookies and cut
Paper dolls and watched chickadees
And played checkers and ate scrambled eggs and
Took our time on the stairs
And you never told me you were dying.

I wanted the chance to say goodbye.

*Lindsay O.*

## Try this:

- *Think of someone you care deeply about (they might still be alive). Using Lindsay's phrase "I remember . . . we" and her style of linking one thing to another, write out the things you have done with this person as quickly as you can.*

- *Write in the same way using the second person "you" instead of "we."*

- *Borrow any line and write as quickly as you can all that the line brings to mind.*

- *Write about whatever this poem brings to mind for you.*

Scholastic Professional Books    *100 Quickwrites* by Linda Rief

# What is it about my grandpa?

What is it about my grandpa
That makes me break down
Sobbing
In the middle of a writing conference with my English teacher?

His warm smile of love
Never too busy to carry my burdens

His frequent and generous hugs
A joke to brighten the day

A life of giving his joy, his love
And now the cross he never wanted to put upon our shoulders

Even in death
He is the one still whispering
I love you

*Hannah L.*

## Try this:

- *For 2–3 minutes, write as quickly as you can all that this poem brings to mind for you.*
- *Borrow any line and write as quickly and as specifically as you can all that comes to mind, letting the line lead your thinking.*

Scholastic Professional Books     *100 Quickwrites* by Linda Rief

# He is my Great-Grandfather

He lives in Wisconsin
I live in New Hampshire
He is old
I am young
He is lonely
I am too

He is the one who put the
worm on my fishing pole
I am the one who threw the
line into the water
He is the one who helped me
bring in my first fish
I am the one who thought it
was a great blue whale
When in reality it was a five inch sunfish

He is the one I love
He is the one I always will

He is my great-grandfather
I am his great-grandson

*Toby M.*

## Try this:

- *Think about someone you like to do things with and write as quickly as you can for 2–3 minutes all that comes to mind when you think of that person and all you do together*

- *Try writing about that person using the contrast of "he" and "I" or "she" and "I."*

- *Think of a grandparent and write as quickly and as specifically as you can, the things you do together.*

Scholastic Professional Books     *100 Quickwrites* by Linda Rief

# Don't You See

"It's just a drink," he says.
But it's really bottled-up rage,
Waiting to explode
And drown my world
In delirium and hatred.
When unleashed,
This simple drink
Destroys families
Shatters lives
And etches nightmares
That beg to be forgotten.

*Zack S.*

## Try this:

- *For 2–3 minutes, write as quickly as you can all that Zack's words bring to mind.*
- *Borrow any line, including perhaps the title, and write as quickly and as specifically as you can all that comes to mind, letting the line lead your thinking.*

Scholastic Professional Books   *100 Quickwrites* by Linda Rief

# Fear

I've never known fear before
Not in its truest sense
I was afraid in World War II
I was afraid in Korea and Vietnam
But now
I've lost fifty pounds
I'm always cold
Always
And now all my hair is gone because of the chemo
My hands are yellow and my breaths are distant and painful
Each one fills the room with the heavy stench of death
The tears running down my pale cheeks can
Now only begin to witness my fear
And the apathetic nurses—who pretend to care—
I know they don't
They'll come in to change my bedpan and ask me
How I feel
And I'll say How do I feel? Like crap. I feel
Like crap. Look at me.
Then they screw on a fake smile
And tell me I look fine
But they don't know
And I am afraid—in the word's truest sense
But I wish desperately that once again
Fear would be merely a distant acquaintance
But now I ache with words I cannot find
And now
I have fear

*Ben H.*

## Try this:

- *For 2–3 minutes, write as quickly as you can all that Ben's words bring to mind for you.*

- *Borrow any line and write as quickly and as specifically as you can all that comes to mind, letting the line lead your thinking.*

- *Ben is writing from his grandfather's point of view, but this really shows Ben's fear also for his grandfather. Writing from the point of view of someone you care deeply about, using the first-person "I," the second-person "you," or the third-person "he/she," write out as quickly and as specifically as you can all that you think that person fears or worries about.*

Scholastic Professional Books      *100 Quickwrites* by Linda Rief

# Old

**I**

When I grow old I'll keep occupied.
I'll jog every day, and I'll keep my stride.
I'll never play bingo after sixty-five;
While others die out, I'll be coming alive.
I won't sulk in chairs saying, "Bottoms up!"
Alcohol will never, ever fill my cup.
I won't be caught
    With grandfather clocks
    Or rocking chairs
    Or holes in my socks.
I won't be seen
    In thirty foot cars
    Or smoking a pipe—
    Not even cigars.
I will not move to
    Tampa Beach
    Or Miami Bay
    Or anywhere
    Where they sit all day.
When I grow old, I want to be known,
As *the crazy old man* living down the road.

**II**

I will never, ever grow old.
I'll always stay so young and bold.
I'll never get
    Dry wrinkled skin
    Or creaky bones
    Or a double chin.
My hair will never turn white or gray.
I will not sit in a chair all day.
I won't become so tired and slow,
Even when it nears my time to go.

It makes me shiver as if I'm cold,
Every time I realize,
I *will* grow old.

*Matt F.*

## Try this:

- *Write as quickly and as specifically as you can all that this poem brings to mind.*
- *Borrow any line and write as quickly as you can, capturing everything that comes to mind.*
- *Write out all those things that worry you, concern you, or bother you about growing old yourself, or that you see in someone else.*

Scholastic Professional Books    *100 Quickwrites* by Linda Rief

# Early Risers

I leap down the creaky chilly stairs, trying to keep up with my nose. The aroma of fresh bread floats up to make sure I'm awake.

I lift the blue and white cloth covering the bread and slice a piece. I slather on butter and homemade strawberry jam. The butter melts instantly. The bread is just hours old. I perch at the window and peer out to find the creator of this mouth-watering bread—Grandpa.

Even before the chickens wake up, Grandpa starts another day of hard work in the fields. The sun is just peaking over the corn stalks. I see Grandpa as he bends down and throws the weeds over his shoulders. Farmers call this "walking the beans." Grandpa, with just 77 years gone by, still is doing the job of a young man.

I run upstairs and jump into my holey blue jeans, stiff from last week's dirt still ground into them. I slip on the shirt that mom says makes me look like a "ragamuffin." But do I care? No! I rush even though it is only 6:30 a.m. The day is being wasted. I'm not going to waste another minute of it, as I dance out to help Grandpa.

*Marianne S.*

## Try this:

- *For 2–3 minutes, write as quickly as you can all that this piece of writing brings to mind for you.*
- *Think about someone you really enjoy doing something with, either now, or when you were little, and write as quickly and as specifically as you can about the things you do/did together.*

Scholastic Professional Books    *100 Quickwrites* by Linda Rief

# The Nursing Home

They reach out
  wrinkled,
    dying hands
  in desperation,
to touch
  swiftly passing people.
I see
  their pain,
 but
  am scared
    by vacant eyes,
  and walk by.
I hear stories
  of lives
    lived long ago,
 but
  do not want
    to get involved.
So
  I listen,
    out-of-place,
  to tales issuing
    from gaping mouths,
and leave
  with guilt
    and relief.

*Karen G.*

## Try this:

- *For 2–3 minutes, write as quickly and as specifically as you can all that this poem brings to mind for you.*
- *Borrow any line and write as quickly as you can, letting the line lead your thinking.*
- *Describe any time you have felt guilt or relief in an uncomfortable situation.*

Scholastic Professional Books    *100 Quickwrites* by Linda Rief

# Penny

Her little eyes peer,
Waiting for my glance.
Tail wiggles,
Ears perk.
Sad eyes stare me down.
Guilt sinks in,
And I become a slave
To throw and fetch.
I throw, she fetches.
I throw, she fetches.
I try to escape to the house,
But those eyes drag me back.
Those adorable, irresistible eyes.
Yes, her little tipped ears
And her incessantly wagging tail
Can make a person's conscience act.
But her eyes can imprison you
In a never-ending game
Of throw and fetch.
Throw and fetch.

*Kerri B.*

## Try this:

- *For 2–3 minutes, write as quickly and as specifically as you can all that this poem brings to mind for you.*
- *Borrow any line and write as quickly as you can, letting the line lead your thinking.*

Scholastic Professional Books    *100 Quickwrites* by Linda Rief

# Cooling Out

The air is sharp in my lungs. Steam rises off Ralph's back as I walk him out. I pull up his cooler as it slides to one side. It's green plaid with so many patches it could pass as a quilt. The sun is setting behind tall black pines that cut into the rose gray sky like knives.

I try to match Ralph's long strides. It hurts. My tall black boots are holding in nine blisters. I reach up to smooth down a mane that demands falling to the right. I hear the feed cart being pushed down the aisle. It's feeding time. Ralph makes a strange deep noise in his chest. He's hungry. He's worked hard and he's tired.

We jumped. I try to bring back the feeling of sailing over jumps higher than Ralph's shoulder. I can't. There's nothing that can make you fly except an oxer or a trekener. He nuzzles my shoulder, bringing me back with a jolt. His huge eyes plead for apple slices. Ralph's breath is not coming in puffs anymore. We're done.

*Rebecca K.*

## Try this:

- *For 2–3 minutes, write as quickly as you can about all that Rebecca's words bring to mind for you.*

- *Think of a moment when you worked hard, and quickly describe that moment with as many sensory details as you can (training an animal, playing a sport, making music, etc.).*

Scholastic Professional Books    *100 Quickwrites* by Linda Rief

# Released

Jonas stared at him. "Release is always like that? For people who break the rules three times? *For the Old? Do they kill the Old, too?*"

*The Giver, p.153  Lois Lowry*

*R*elease, *I think. We released* him. *Two weeks ago the term meant nothing. Now its meaning is all too clear.*

"The cancer spread to his pancreas," *my mother tries to soothe.* "There was nothing they could do." *Never nothing, I think, looking down at the beautiful cat that was once my pet. Never nothing. But when I speak I am neutral and even-keeled.*

"Did they ask first?"

"They called at 11:30. I told them they could . . ." *she trails off. I try to remember,* 11:30, where was I?

"It's better this way. It's an easier way to go." *Easier for whom? Society, or the cat? I don't speak.*

---

*My sister sits on the steps, crying. The words to Mary J. Blige's "No More Drama" run through my head like the stock prices on the giant Wall Street ticker-belt.* We murdered him; we created the drama. No, not we, mom. She said yes. She said, "Go . . ." *Tears cloud my thoughts and vision.* Easier for whom?

---

*I sit in the garage, cradling Redbeard. His body is stiff and cold, though his fur is soft. I scratch behind his ears, just like I used to. Inside the house I hear my sister giggling at the thought of a puppy.* "Where would we get it?" *she squeals excitedly.* Fair weather friend. How can you talk of a puppy?

*Mom pushes the garage door open and sits on the floor beside me.* "He looks just like he used to when he was asleep." *Her fingers brush his whiskers. I want to push her away, but I don't. Something won't let me.* No. He squinted his eyes and smiled when he slept.

"Hmmm," *I grunt in reply.* This is my cat, but I don't know him. He isn't here, or any other earthly place. Redbeard isn't a body; he's a being, and that being is gone. He's the happy meow that woke me in the morning, the soothing purr when I felt bad. Why wasn't I there for him?

*I shift the body in my arms. In my head I talk to him, the real him, the one I knew all my life, before the release.* Redbeard, I love you.

*Natasha P.*

## Try this:

- *For 2–3 minutes, write as quickly as you can all that this memory brings to mind for you.*
- *Think of a time you were saddened by the loss of a pet and describe as quickly and as specifically as you can all that you remember.*

Scholastic Professional Books     *100 Quickwrites* by Linda Rief

# My Sky

We were outside
in the street
me and some other kids
kicking the ball
before dinner
and Sky was
chasing chasing chasing
with his feet going
every which way
and his tail
wag-wag-wagging
and his mouth
Slob-slob-slobbering
and he was
all over the place
smiling and wagging
and slobbering
and making
us laugh
and my dad
came walking up the street
he was way down there
near the end
I could see him
after he got off the bus
and he was walk-walk-
　　walking
and I saw him wave
and he called out
"Hey there, son!"

and so I didn't see
the car
coming from the other way
until someone else—
one of the big kids—
called out
"Car!"
and I turned around
and saw a
*blue car blue car*
*splattered with mud*
*speeding down the road*

And I saw Sky
going after the ball
wag-wag-wagging
his tail
and I called him
"Sky! Sky!"
and he turned his
head
but it was too late
because the
*blue car blue car*
*splattered with mud*
hit Sky
*thud thud thud*
and kept on going
in such a hurry
so fast

so many miles to go
it couldn't even stop
and
Sky
was just there
in the road
lying on his side
with his legs bent funny
and his side heaving
and he looked up at me
and I said
"Sky! Sky! Sky!"
and then my dad
was there
and he lifted Sky
out of the road
and laid him on the grass

and
Sky
closed his eyes
and
he
never
opened
them
again
ever.

*From* Love That Dog
*by Sharon Creech*

## Try this:

- *For 2–3 minutes, write out as quickly as you can all that this poem brings to mind for you.*

- *Borrow any line and write as quickly and as specifically as you can for 2–3 minutes.*

Scholastic Professional Books　　*100 Quickwrites* by Linda Rief

# What the Pony Taught Us

Walk if you must.
Canter when you can.
Jump high and strong
And with great joy.

Eat heartily.
Shed abundantly.
Love greatly.
Listen well.

Be wary but ready.
Trust when the trust comes.
Learn to give in.

Open your eyes to beauty
Beyond long legs, perfect hair.
Make them see beauty
That is only yours.

Don't fret over words.
Mostly we cannot say
All there is to say.
We need also a touch, a look,
A slight tilt of the head . . .

Take the weight of your saddle
And bear proudly your friends.
Learn what you are asked to learn
As best as you can.

At the end of the day,
Rest peacefully
And wait patiently,
And know certainly
That we will ride
Together again.

*Martha B. Kane*

## Try this:

- *For 2–3 minutes, write as quickly as you can all that Martha's words bring to mind for you.*

- *For 2–3 minutes, write as quickly as you can all you have learned from an animal, domesticated or wild.*

- *Borrow any line and write as quickly and as specifically as you can, letting the line lead your thinking.*

Scholastic Professional Books     *100 Quickwrites* by Linda Rief

# Knoxville, Tennessee

I always like summer
best
you can eat fresh corn
from daddy's garden
and okra
and greens
and cabbage
and lots of
barbecue
and buttermilk
and homemade ice-cream
at the church picnic
and listen to
gospel music
outside
at the church
homecoming
and go to the mountains with
your grandmother
and go barefooted
and be warm
all the time
not only when you go to bed
and sleep

*Nikki Giovanni from* Knoxville, Tennessee

## Try this:

- *For 2–3 minutes, write as quickly as you can all that this poem brings to mind for you.*
- *Borrow the line, "I always like _____ best," and insert a person, place, thing, event, season, etc. Write as quickly and as specifically as you can to describe (in a list format, if you prefer) all those things you like best.*

# P.S. 81 The Bronx

We sat on the basement floor that June
afternoon
because it was cooler
than the oven
we called our classroom.
I pressed my steaming face
against the cold
ceramic tiles.
Except for the occasional
thwump and bang of the boiler
and the monotonous
droning of our teacher's voice
silence surrounded us.
Our thoughts floated away
on rivers of sweat.
The teacher drawled on
"Repeat after me
a noun is a person, place, or
thing. . . ."
Trancelike we repeated,

"A noun is a person, place, or
thing. A noun is a . . . a . . ."
beach,
white glistening sand
a cool breeze
clear water licking
at my toes.
A pronoun is me...
me at that beach.
Spray mists my body.
I inhale
drifts of sticky salt.
I lick my lips.
Sweat rolls down my face. My face
pressed against
cold
hard
ceramic
tiles.

*Naomi S.*

## Try this:

- *Think of a time when you drifted away from what you should have been concentrating on (a teacher's lesson, a parent's lecture, a religious sermon, etc.) and write as quickly as you can for 2–3 minutes about all that you were thinking or imagining.*

- *Borrow a line from Naomi's poem and write for 2–3 minutes all that comes to mind.*

- *For 2–3 minutes, write as quickly as you can all that this piece brings to mind for you.*

Scholastic Professional Books    *100 Quickwrites* by Linda Rief

# The Dunes

The dunes, shadowed by scattered trees—oaks, juniper, pine, hemlock, birch—glistened in the sunlight. Mountains of sand burned hot under my naked feet. The dunes eventually flattened out into a beach nestled near the Great Lake.

My brother and I ran up to the top of the dune and gazed out . . . out to see . . . powerplants? The powerplants of Gary, Indiana, spewing their chemicals from smokestacks.

The sight surprised me, like tasting brussel sprouts for the first time. I wanted to spit those smokestacks away, but the bitter taste hung in my mouth.

I started down the dune, faster, faster—speeding until I tripped and fell, standing, laughing, and spitting the sand out of my mouth as easily as those chimneys spit soot.

In two hours this beach would be quiet, leaving the sun to set, the end of the work bells to sound at the powerplants, and the downtown traffic to build up in Chicago. Only in the park would it be quiet.

The silent park fell asleep all at once, leaving only the animals to roam. As I lay down to sleep, I thought of the millions of spots like this park that are being destroyed every day. Maybe this would be the last time I would be able to see such blue skies, breathe such clean air, and swim in Lake Michigan. Or would the taste of brussel sprouts ruin everything? Will that taste ever go away?

*Jeremy G.*

## Try this:

- *For 2–3 minutes, write as quickly as you can all that this piece brings to mind for you.*
- *Think of a place you have really enjoyed in the natural world, and describe as quickly and as specifically as you can all you remember of the sensory details of the place.*
- *Think of other natural wonders and a clean environment, and write as quickly and as specifically as you can about your worries for the future of the natural world.*

Scholastic Professional Books    *100 Quickwrites* by Linda Rief

# Watermelon Day

It's a watermelon day.
Nothing left to do but soak up summer.
Feel the sun up and down your spine,
Warm and tingling in a reassuring way.
Laze around and dream of cool water down your back,
Cold lemonade down your throat,
And juicy sweet watermelon on your tongue.
Lie in a hammock and sway
In a breeze you conjure in your mind,
Imagining a checkered blanket beside a cat-tailed pond.
The blanket is covered with pickles and pasta and ants,
And slightly burned pork chops.
Think about catching your imagination's fireflies,
While you lie in a freshly mowed field.
Listen to the crickets as they sing their August song.
Watch as the watermelon day passes you by.
And love life while you have it.

*Rebecca K.*

## Try this:

- *For 2–3 minutes, write as quickly as you can all that this poem brings to mind.*

- *Borrow a line and write as quickly and specifically as you can from that line.*

- *Write as quickly as you can all of the sights, sounds, smells, tastes, and touches that come to mind when you think of summer.*

Scholastic Professional Books    *100 Quickwrites* by Linda Rief

# Fog

5 a.m.
the earliness of the morning weighed me down
like water in a cup
the harbor was still
so still the silence hummed
the fog rested at the rocky entrance of the harbor
billowing veils
paused
restrained
at the red buoy that sat angled in the water
then
like a bag of sugar bursting
it was released
floating
drifting
unrolling before me over the stillness
it surrounded me
I could only see the water
a cobalt gray
a red flag
sagging at the top of a sailboat
I breathed in the fog
it was cool and refreshing like October rain
I bathed in the calm
And then
My heart dropped
I remembered the sun would come up today

*Janet M.*

## Try this:

- *Think of the sights, sounds, and smells of a quiet place or a rowdy place you love going, and write as quickly and as specifically as you can about this place.*
- *Borrow any line from this poem and write as quickly as you can, anywhere it leads you.*

Scholastic Professional Books     *100 Quickwrites* by Linda Rief

# School Days

In Maine I've learned . . .
How to sail my grandparents' sunfish boat
The backstroke, freestyle, and the deadman's float
How to catch a pickerel on a rod and reel
How to enjoy red hotdogs every third meal

In Maine I've learned . . .
How to walk through a swamp and burn off a leach
To lay in the sun or dig traps in the beach
How to dive through the water or flip from the float
To ski on one ski from my grandfather's boat

In Maine I've learned . . .
How to steer a canoe
Or if it flips, what I'm to do
How to catch a turtle with just my bare hands
Or build castles and cities with water and sand

In Maine I've learned . . .
To absorb what I see
And how to relax and just be me

*Trisha W.*

## Try this:

- *For 2–3 minutes, write as quickly as you can all that this poem brings to mind for you.*
- *Borrow any line and write as quickly and as specifically as you can, letting the line lead your thinking.*
- *Borrow the line "In Maine, I've learned . . .," substituting any other "place" (state, country, grade level, sport, club or hobby, etc.) for Maine, if you choose to, and write as quickly and as specifically as you can for 2–3 minutes.*

Scholastic Professional Books    *100 Quickwrites* by Linda Rief

# Autumn

I want to mention
summer ending
without meaning the death
of somebody loved

or even the death
of the trees.
Today in the market
I heard a mother say

Look at the pumpkins,
it's finally autumn!
And the child didn't think
of the death of her mother

which is due before her own
but tasted the sound
of the words on her clumsy tongue:
pumpkin; autumn.

Let the eye enlarge
with all it beholds.
I want to celebrate
color, how one red leaf

flickers like a match
held to a dry branch,
and the whole world goes up
in orange and gold.

*from* Heroes in Disguise *by Linda Pastan*

## Try this:

- *For 2–3 minutes, write as quickly as you can all that this poem brings to mind for you.*
- *Borrow any line and write as quickly and as specifically as you can, letting the line lead your thinking.*
- *Think of autumn or any other season and describe the sights, sounds, smells, and events that you like most about that season.*

( 83 )

# Buttermints

It doesn't get much better—
buttermints on a wind-blown day,
when the iced October air
mingles them in your mouth
and makes you want to live forever.

Against the sapphire sky,
when bright leaves
fall like embers from the trees,
reach out and catch just one leaf
before it hits the ground.
Then make a wish.

There is so much to ask for—
a hundred prismed diamonds,
a team of sable stallions,
or a ladder to the moon.

Yet all you'll wish for
is another autumn day,
just like this one,
and one more
pocketful of buttermints.

*Amity Gaige from* We Are a Thunderstorm

This poem is best read on a cool October day, after a few buttermints have been given to each student.

## Try this:

- *For 2–3 minutes, write as quickly as you can all that this poem brings to mind for you.*
- *Borrow any line and write as quickly and as specifically as you can, letting the line lead your thinking.*

Scholastic Professional Books    *100 Quickwrites* by Linda Rief

# Walking Down a Stone Driveway

Piles of gold line the loose stones,
Curled at the edges,
Huddling together for warmth in the cold, crisp fall air.
The drive looks like a tunnel of gold
Sweeping together at the top
With pieces of brilliant blue tracing through the branches.
The moss slowly crawls down the stone floor,
Slowly unrolling a carpet
For the final clash of colors,
Before the ancient ceilings crumble into brown piles.

And people drive by
So fast.

*Dana S.*

## Try this:

- *Write as quickly as you can anything this poem brings to mind for you.*
- *Think of a single sight that either pleases or bothers you and describe that sight as quickly and as specifically as you can for 2–3 minutes.*
- *Borrow any line from the poem and write as quickly as you can, letting the line lead you.*
- *Borrow the line "Huddling together for warmth" or "And people drive by so fast" and write from either of these lines as quickly as you can.*

Scholastic Professional Books     *100 Quickwrites* by Linda Rief

# Through the Night Window I Imagine
## What Could Be Hidden

A delicious horizon,
    Like smoked whitefish on deli-wrap
    Beckons to me.
A Great Blue Heron breezes on grayish, icy water.
Straggling, gnarled fingers struggle for a place
    To clutch the faulty ground halfway across the bay.
Houses scatter across the distant shore,
    Bread crumbs for the birds.
Tiny diamonds of light pinpoint
    Quickly darkening gray-blue shadows.

I turn—delicious.

*Nahanni R.*

## Try this:

- *Write as quickly and as specifically as you can all that this poem brings to mind for you.*
- *Borrow any line and write as quickly as possible, letting the line lead your thinking.*
- *Think of a place, sight, or thing you enjoy and describe as specifically as you can all that comes to mind.*

Scholastic Professional Books     *100 Quickwrites* by Linda Rief

# Black River

the air bites my lungs in iciness
as I exhale a soft veil of swirling mist drifts
    into the air
and is lost in the deep density of the night
my heart beats in excitement
the bright crimson berries on the weeping
    crab tree
encrusted in a crystal cocoon
contrast softly with the pure white snow
icy crust
crackling and crunching under the rubber
    soles of my boots
brings something from deep inside me into
    the open
I laugh
nothing is funny
my sled is poised
set to go
glancing down the hill I see a sleek flat slope
the light from the house slowly diminishing
into an endless black hole
I take a running start
I race down the hill against wind and time
once gusty and sharp
the wind is now a smooth black river
it hits my face
drying my eyes
filling my ears with rushing sound
it slides over my body and is left on the snow
I slide for an eternity

forever I am going into the deepest
    blackest river
cold
forbidding
but feeling warm and secure
in my down parka
the sled slows to a stop
I lie there in a deep sleep
every muscle in my body
gives a last grind and drops
like a wet rag
snow
nipping at my waist
cutting at my wrist
the tears
once warm and streaming
now frozen on my face
I stand up and look around
in one direction
that black forbidding river lays before me
clean and cold
I can imagine the crisp air
flying past white diamonds
in the sky
Where do I go?
I smile
shrug
and head uphill for another run

*Janet M.*

## Try this:

- *For 2–3 minutes, write as quickly and as specifically as you can all that this experience brings to mind for you (could be sledding, mountain biking, hiking, playing football. . .).*
- *Borrow any line and write as specifically and as quickly as you can wherever the line leads you.*

Scholastic Professional Books    *100 Quickwrites* by Linda Rief

# February Air

Bitter cold air
Nips
At my face
I tingle all over
Like a first love
Snow gusts and whirls
Chunks of sugar cubes
Dissolving in drifts of snow
Knee deep
My footsteps
Crunch
Like crackling
Cold cereal
Twisted branches
Follow me home
I walk fast
In the darkness
Of the night
Snowflakes of memory
Guiding me home

*Paula M.*

## Try this:

- *Write as quickly as you can all that Paula's poem brings to mind for you.*
- *Think of any season you especially like and write as quickly and as specifically as you can all of the sensory details that come to mind.*
- *Borrow any line and write as quickly and as specifically as you can, letting the line lead your thinking.*

Scholastic Professional Books    *100 Quickwrites* by Linda Rief

# And Spring Whispers Utopia

Robin redbreasted sunrise
Green velvet carpets the burlap earth
The sun blows buttercup pollen
Flowers sprout in paisley patterns
The world is rain green

Midday dances above

Noon lingers
Purple shadows finger toward the horizon
The evening air breathes musk
Fireflies swim in tall grass
Night sings crickets and hums mosquitoes

And spring whispers *Utopia*

*Abigail C.*

## Try this:

- *Think of a season you love and try to capture the sensory details of that season as quickly as you can for 2–3 minutes.*
- *Borrow any line and write as quickly and as specifically as you can all that the line brings to mind for you, letting the line lead your thinking.*

Scholastic Professional Books    *100 Quickwrites* by Linda Rief

# Crossing the River

Sitting with me
On a hillside
Looking down and across
A green valley,
My father
Once said to me
*You never step*
*Into the same river twice.*

I nodded
Like I understood
What he said.
That was then.
When I step
Onto a soccer field
Or out the door to school
Or open any book
Now
Now I know what he meant.

*Jesse S.*

## Try this:

- *For 2–3 minutes, write as quickly as you can all that this poem brings to mind for you.*

- *Borrow any line and write as quickly and as specifically as you can, letting the line lead your thinking.*

- *Thinking of the line "You never step into the same river twice," write as quickly as you can all that comes to mind.*

Scholastic Professional Books    *100 Quickwrites* by Linda Rief

# Unknown Soldier

He is the unknown soldier
Fighting a war for himself
Hoping for a rank above
Social security number
Or alphabetized name

Somewhere
Between the alleys of Harlem
And the dirt roads of untitled towns
He was lost

Old men in pressed shirts
And shined shoes
Gaze at their blurred reflections
Of wrinkled faces and forgotten goals
They salute the lost cause hidden with layers
Of aged hope defeated by bureaucracy

So the soldier presses on
Gasping for clean air
In the dust that he raises

*Duncan H.*

## Try this:

- *For 2–3 minutes, write as quickly as you can all that Duncan's words bring to mind for you.*
- *Borrow any line and write as quickly and as specifically as you can all that comes to mind, letting the line lead your thinking.*
- *Duncan wrote this piece after visiting Washington, D.C., and seeing so many homeless men and women on the streets, many of whom were Vietnam veterans. Think about the images of people or places you have seen that disturbed you, and write as quickly and as specifically as you can all that comes to mind.*

Scholastic Professional Books     *100 Quickwrites* by Linda Rief

# Charlotte's Web

Twenty-eight third graders sprawled
on the carpet
in our blustery January classroom.
Anticipating some unknown feat,
we counted the seconds
with the newscaster
and cheered at the bursts of flame,
awed by how quickly
the shuttle hit the sky.
I was unaware
that anything went wrong
until someone gasped,
children's voices hushed,
and newscasters broke the silence.

Kathy cried and cried and I
hated her for it,
the same sorrow she had shown
when we watched *Charlotte's Web* in the second grade.
She wallowed in it, her grief,
and took the whole kleenex box,
while I could not bring myself to shed a tear.

*Lindsay O.*

## Try this:

- *For 2–3 minutes, write as quickly as you can all that this poem brings to mind for you.*
- *Borrow any line and write as quickly as you can, letting the line lead your thinking.*
- *Lindsay describes an immediate reaction to a moment that turned to disaster (the explosion of the Challenger space shuttle). Think of any personal, national, or international moment that had the same impact of surprise on you, and describe that moment as quickly and as specifically as you can.*

Scholastic Professional Books     *100 Quickwrites* by Linda Rief

# Only Human

He sits over subway grates
Legs tucked up against his body
Wearing dirt-smudged khakis
And a ripped flannel shirt
That homeless man
Who reaches out his hand
And motions to a pan of pennies and nickels
That homeless man
Who people awkwardly step around
Not bothering to give a second glance
Like being poor is a disease
That can be caught
And spread
He sits
Like a stray dog
Flea-covered and matted
At night he curls in doorways
Aching with empty stomach pains
He is a veteran
A grandfather
A businessman
In need of love and care
He is a human being
Not a beggar
He speaks nothing but one plea
I beg of you
Feed me

*Kerri B.*

## Try this:

- *For 2–3 minutes, write as quickly as you can all that these words bring to mind for you.*
- *Borrow any line and write as quickly as you can, letting the line lead your thinking.*
- *Write as quickly as you can about those things in the world that you "step around" and often try to ignore because they make you uncomfortable.*

Scholastic Professional Books    *100 Quickwrites* by Linda Rief

# The White Flakes

(On reading *Schindler's List*)

Low creeping fog spreads
Across the ground, like a vine
Sucking the life
Out of the air
A shiver blows
From barracks to barracks
These are no hotels
But holding tanks of fuel for
The furnace
Each living
Breathing
Human
Turned to puffs of smoke under
The night's sky
Children play
In the endless snowflakes
Catching them on their tongues
Only stopping
Because these little white flakes
Never melt

*Ben W.*

## Try this:

- *For 2–3 minutes, write as quickly as you can all that this poem brings to mind for you.*
- *Borrow any line and write as quickly and as specifically as you can, letting the line lead your thinking.*
- *Think of a book you've read that changed your life. Start your writing with the phrase, "On reading . . ." and describe a moment in the book that affected your thoughts, beliefs, or feelings.*

Scholastic Professional Books     *100 Quickwrites* by Linda Rief

# Reverence

Seeming to fall from the sky,
news passed from fated messengers
playing hot potato with
tragedy.
Exchanging no words, only
nervous glances of expectant sympathy,
we searched in vain
for *the right words*,
any words. Found nothing but
Amanda's tear,
a muffled cough, the static monotone
of the P.A. system drilling into us
information we suddenly were too innocent
to absorb.
Hovering at the edge of the sidewalk,
there was almost a comfort
in silence,
a muted acknowledgement
of respect.
Beyond class, beyond clique, beyond every moral prejudice,
gym teacher and sophomore alike
became comforter,
where *the right word* was obsolete.
If nothing else,
perhaps we will take from this, the discovery
that we're all a little more human,
that we can each feel pain,
each lower ourselves to cry.

*Lindsay O.*

## Try this:

- *For 2–3 minutes, write as quickly as you can all that Lindsay's words bring to mind for you.*

- *Borrow any line and write as quickly and as specifically as you can all that comes to mind, letting the line lead your thinking.*

- *Think of news that left you speechless and write as quickly and as specifically as you can all that you remember happening and feeling at that moment.*

Scholastic Professional Books    *100 Quickwrites* by Linda Rief

# Seabrook Nuclear Power Plant
# To Whom It May Concern:

We
Students
Not registered voters
Not taxpayers
Without any reason to believe we can make a difference
For some reason decided
That although we don't have influence
We will never say never
The future is ours
But the toxic waste
In the fine print
Is yours
This may simply be a list of personless names to you
But it's more than that
It's our way of saying
You can't do this
Even if you disregard this
As we expect you will
Even if you put Seabrook into operation
As we expect you will
Even if you give us your toxic waste or your "minimal" chance
Of annihilation
You can't forget
An unimportant minority called
The future
That cries out to be saved
From your dogmatism
Your propaganda
Your madness

*Sandy P.*

## Try this:

- *For 2–3 minutes, write as quickly as you can all that this piece of writing brings to mind for you.*

- *Borrow any line and write as quickly and as specifically as you can all that the line brings to mind, letting the line lead your thinking.*

- *Write as quickly and as specifically as you can about a world issue that you feel strongly about.*

Scholastic Professional Books     *100 Quickwrites* by Linda Rief

# A Hollow Smile

My street filled with people
Glancing my way.

My school filled with students
What will they say?

I look at my life.
Will this be my last breath?

When my friends look at me
They see inescapable death.

Once people know my illness
They pretend that they care.

So I smile, I laugh
But my heart is not there.

My hopes, my dreams, my life
They slowly all fade.

Life is not easy
With HIV/AIDS.

*Dave H.*

## Try this:

- *For 2–3 minutes, write as quickly as you can all that this poem brings to mind.*
- *Borrow any line and write quickly and specifically as much as you can, letting the line lead your thinking.*
- *In what way has life not been easy for you or someone you know? Write as quickly and specifically as you can about this topic.*

Scholastic Professional Books    *100 Quickwrites* by Linda Rief

# Little Boys

Little boys aren't all made
of puppy dog tails
   and frogs and snails.
Nowadays they're made
   of ninja turtles
   GI Joes, beebee guns
   and karate clothes.
Little girls aren't all made
of sugar and spice
   and everything nice.
Today they're made
of street-corner Barbies
   permanent hair dyes
   skeleton earrings
   and dark black lies.
Parents contribute
   when kids are young

giving them TVs
   and dangerous guns.
But as kids grow up
   and still
Keep these
   bad morals till
Society becomes
   a black hole
For criminals who take
   their mighty toll.
Nowadays, boys aren't made
   of puppy dog tails
   and frogs and snails
And girls aren't made
   of sugar and spice
   and everything nice.

*Emma T.*

## Try this:

- *For 2–3 minutes, write as quickly as you can all that this poem brings to mind for you.*
- *Borrow any line and write as quickly and as specifically as you can, letting the line lead your thinking.*
- *Write as quickly and as specifically as you can about how you agree or disagree with Emma's contention about today's little boys and little girls.*

# And So It Goes

And so it goes,
That death is justified by the declaration of war.

What separates the soldier from the murderer?
What separates murder from government executions?
Why is the enemy's death rejoiced, when it's also
                                    the death of God's child?
Why do I blame murder on those who are willing to sacrifice
                                    their lives for mine?

How might the words of one man rationalize the demise of thousands?
And different words from the same man, condemn the killing of others?

Is it wrong, immoral, to ask these questions, knowing that I am not
                                    strong enough to protest the answers?
I am not the first to ponder these questions,
                        nor will I be the last,
                                for so it goes,
                                        and forever will.

*Duncan H.*

## Try this:

- *For 2–3 minutes, write as quickly as you can all that this piece of writing brings to mind for you.*

- *Borrow any line and write as quickly and as specifically as you can all that the line brings to mind, letting the line lead your thinking.*

- *What do you think Duncan is trying to say in this poem? What makes you think that? In what ways do you agree or disagree?*

Scholastic Professional Books     *100 Quickwrites* by Linda Rief

# Embassy

As evening fell the day's oppression lifted;
Far peaks came into focus; it had rained;
Across wide lawns and cultured flowers drifted
The conversation of the highly trained.

Two gardeners watched them pass and priced their shoes:
A chauffeur waited, reading in the drive,
For them to finish their exchange of views;
It seemed a picture of the private life.

Far off, no matter what good they intended,
The armies waited for a verbal error
With all the instruments for causing pain;

And on the issue of their charm depended
A land laid waste, with all its young men slain,
Its women weeping, and its towns in terror.

*W. H. Auden*

## Try this:

- *For 2–3 minutes, write as quickly as you can all that this piece of writing brings to mind for you.*

- *Borrow any line and write as quickly and as specifically as you can all that the line brings to mind, letting the line lead your thinking.*

- *What do you think Auden is trying to say in this poem? What makes you think that? In what ways do you agree or disagree?*

Scholastic Professional Books    *100 Quickwrites* by Linda Rief

# The Game

Plastic soldiers march on the floor
Off to fight a terrible war.

The green troops charge. The grey side falls.
Guns splatter bullets on the walls.

Tanks move in. Jet fighters zoom
Dropping bombs all over the room.

All the soldiers are dead but two.
The game is over. The war is through.

The plastic soldiers are put away.
What other game is there to play?

*Myra Cohn Livingston*

## Try this:

- *For 2–3 minutes, write as quickly as you can all that this piece of writing brings to mind for you.*

- *Borrow any line and write as quickly and as specifically as you can all that the line brings to mind, letting the line lead your thinking.*

- *What do you think Livingston is trying to say in this poem? What makes you think that? In what ways do you agree or disagree?*

Scholastic Professional Books    *100 Quickwrites* by Linda Rief

# Dear Mr. President,

My grandmother on the other side of the world has a lemon tree that whispers secrets. She talks to it and gives it water from her own drinking glass. She guesses the branch where lemons will grow next. All the old men and women of her village take good care of their trees. Some have fig trees with shiny leaves. Some have almond trees covered with white blossoms that fall down on the road like snow.

Last night when I watched TV, I felt worried. If the people of the United States could meet Sitti, they'd like her, for sure. You'd like her, too.

My grandmother can read the stars and the moon and the clouds. She can read dreams and tea leaves in the bottom of a cup. She even said she could read good luck on my forehead.

Mr. President, I wish you my good luck in your very hard job. I vote for peace. My grandmother votes with me.

Sincerely,
Mona

This passage is from the picture book *Sitti's Secrets* by Naomi Shihab Nye. It is the story of a young girl who lives in the United States describing a visit to her grandmother in a Palestinian village on the West Bank.

## Try this:

- *For 2–3 minutes, write as quickly as you can all that this letter brings to mind for you.*
- *If you were to write a letter to anyone about a world situation, what might you say to that person in an attempt to convince them of your thinking?*
- *Mona picks one person, her grandmother, to describe to the president in her effort to convince him that war and peace are about human beings, each one special. Who would you pick to describe and to whom? Write about that person as quickly and as specifically as you can.*

Scholastic Professional Books     *100 Quickwrites* by Linda Rief

# Tragedy Strikes Columbine

Flowers stacked
The piles are high
How did they decide
Who was to die?

People arrive
From many places
Horror shows
On students' faces

How did all
Of this start?
Peoples' lives
Now torn apart

Did it all
Erupt from teasing?
Families now
Continue grieving

All students should
Be respected
In order for everyone
To be protected

So maybe Columbine
Should not be
Just another story
Ending in sympathy.

*Kristen C.*

## Try this:

- *For 2–3 minutes, write as quickly as you can all that this poem brings to mind for you.*
- *Borrow any line and write as quickly and as specifically as you can, letting the line lead your thinking.*
- *Think about things that could be done to prevent anger from erupting into violence and write as quickly and as specifically as you can all that comes to mind.*

Scholastic Professional Books    *100 Quickwrites* by Linda Rief

# September 11, 2001   New York City   8:26 a.m.

Each day a tear
For those who died
A prism of loss
Our country cried

    We carry on
    With broken hearts
    What went wrong?
    Where can we start?

Two towers
Struck today
*He who acted*
**Must now pay**

    Reach for the stars
    Go for the gold
    Hang on forever
    Until we grow old

A river of hate
Burns in your eyes
A moment there's hope
Then your fury flies

    Recall that day
    Never forget
    Images stay
    Feelings are set

Be not afraid
Your friends are near
Hold close to you
Those you call dear

    Red for the force
    Of those who passed
    White is the source
    Of trustfulness

Blue for justice
Perseverance
Weakness is worthless
Resolve is ageless

    Look to the stars
    And see their hope
    A day will come
    When you can cope

You must play
The hand you're dealt
But never forget
The way you felt

    United here
    By stars and stripes
    Where life is clear
    We carry on

*Hannah L.*

## Try this:

- *For 2–3 minutes, write as quickly as you can all that comes to mind when you think of September 11th, 2001.*

- *Borrow any line from Hannah's poem and write as quickly and as specifically as you can, letting the line lead your thinking.*

Scholastic Professional Books     *100 Quickwrites* by Linda Rief

# Simple Truths

On one side of the Earth
purple fragrances touch the hands of many
and yellow sunflowers and clear thoughts
grow to new heights.

Crisp white laundry and fresh clean
friendships
Are hung out to dry.

Wars are fought over colored marbles
but amends are made as easily as picking a leaf
from a small apple tree.

Small wars are fought over possession
of toys.
Harsh words are exchanged,
but forgiveness is always asked.
Hard feelings are brushed off like fleas.

On another side of the Earth,
the real war rages on,
no side asking forgiveness.
All that is said, held against a soul.

What people don't realize is the way war
picks at your spirit,
and slowly eats away at it.

What people don't see
is the true beauty of simple words,
and the secret of youth.

What people don't hear
are the tiny words that hold great meaning:
forgiveness; peace.

What people don't acknowledge
is the immature way
adults settle an argument.
Fists fly.
Rude words linger.

What people don't know
they should simply learn
from children.

*Anupama V.*

## Try this:

- *Borrow any line from this poem and write as quickly and as specifically as you can all that the line makes you think about.*
- *Write as quickly as you can all that this poem brings to mind for you.*
- *Write out the "simple truths" that you believe would make this world a better place.*

Scholastic Professional Books    *100 Quickwrites* by Linda Rief

# Let Me Introduce Myself

I wanted to show you who I was
I was happy, angry, laughing, but mostly sad
All at the same time
Thoughts ran through my mind
And cascaded down waterfalls to be lost
    in the murky depth below
The water had to clear

I tried to write a story
To show you
How lost I was, how empty and
    and lonely I felt
But the paragraphs eluded me
Run-on sentences and dialogue of fictional
    characters
Gave way to lies
Nothing was real
And if I couldn't tell myself the truth,
    how could you understand
What I meant to say?
My hand could not write
    the words of my heart

I tried to write a song
I wanted you to understand
How each chord made me feel
How the melody lingered on my mind
Playing games with my soul
But the staff confused me
The quarter notes were plain and simple
And would not speak to a stranger

I wanted you to know me
To hear through my ears
And see through my eyes
Eyes that filled with silent tears
Until they flowed over the edge
And I poured myself into
A poem for you

*Megan G.*

---

## Try this:

- *For 2–3 minutes, write as quickly as you can all that Megan's words bring to mind for you.*
- *Borrow any line and write as quickly and as specifically as you can, letting the line lead your thinking.*
- *Think about the line "Let me introduce myself . . ." and write as quickly and as specifically as you can, letting the line lead your thinking.*

Scholastic Professional Books    *100 Quickwrites* by Linda Rief

# Poetry Was...

Poetry was wading through a knee-deep river
Across a fog-laden path,
The morning call for prayer, or the burning of paddy stalks
After the harvesting, the lovely dark dots of rye
On the plump crust of a homemade country cake,
The smell of fish, a fishing-net spread out
On the courtyard to dry,
And Grandpa's grave under a cluster of bamboo leaves.

*Al Mahmud Bangladesh from "Poetry Was Like This"*
*Translated by Kabir Chowdhury from* This Same Sky. *Selected by Naomi Shihab Nye*

Poetry was searching for Cossacks in the crevices of heavy castle rocks, stones carried by peasants with rounded shoulders, standing solid above the Hessian town of Marburg.

Poetry was in the words of bare-footed Pilipino mothers beckoning naked, dark-skinned children to follow: "Halika dito! Halika dito!" as they scurried the dirt road along the Pasig River.

Poetry was me, a chubby four-year-old, fat fingers pressing periwinkles and mussels, squatting in the sand and incoming wash of the Atlantic Ocean, wondering then, and now, where the tide went and how it knew to come back.

Poetry is peeling birch bark from a tree, imagining myself an indian in soft moccasins . . . it's my grandmother's black braid coiled tightly in a tin box in her top bureau drawer . . .

*Linda Rief*

## Try this:

- *Start with the phrase "Poetry was . . ." or "Poetry is . . ." and add as quickly as you can the most ordinary sights, sounds, and smells that stay with you.*
- *Write for 2–3 minutes about anything that came to mind as you listened to the lines from either piece.*
- *Write for 2–3 minutes about those things you remember imagining, playing, or wondering about as a young child—or still imagine, play, or wonder about today.*

Scholastic Professional Books     *100 Quickwrites* by Linda Rief

# Writing Past Midnight

*insects drone . . . the night draws on . . .*
*I am writing a poem about a barn . . .*

and my room is warm with the breath of horses
and dust from the loft runs in streams down the walls
and somewhere the sound
                    of sheep snoring softly
blends with the hum of computers
                    asleep in their stalls
bundled with bailing wire
                    stanzas
                    are stacked
                    to the ceiling
spiderwebs anchor the edge of my desk to the floor
a small gray verse runs squeaking down one of the rafters

just as the moon floats in through the double barn door

*Alice Schertle from* A Lucky Thing

## Try this:

- *For 2–3 minutes, write as quickly as you can all that this poem brings to mind for you.*
- *Borrow any line and write as quickly and as specifically as you can, letting the line lead your thinking.*

Scholastic Professional Books  *100 Quickwrites* by Linda Rief

# But I'll Be Back Again

"If you are a child who is never told the truth, you begin to make up your own. After my father left, and no one mentioned his name again, I simply made things up about him. When the teacher in fourth grade asked me where he was, I said he was in San Francisco on business. He had been gone since I was four. . . . San Francisco was just an invention of mine, trying to make a father for myself out of nothing. I had no idea where he was or what he was doing.

"They say that to be a writer you must first have an unhappy childhood. I don't know if unhappiness is necessary, but I think maybe some children who have suffered a loss too great for words grow up into writers who are always trying to find those words, trying to find a meaning for the way they have lived. Painters do that. And composers. Everything they have lived is squeezed onto canvas or is penned between the bars of a page of music. It is as if we, as children, just felt the life, then after we grew up we wanted to see it. So we create stories and paintings and music, not so much for the world, as for ourselves." (p.5)

"I did not have a chance to know [my father] or to say goodbye to him, and that is all the loss I needed to become a writer." (p. 7)

"Writing stories has given me the power to change things I could not change as a child. I can make boys into doctors. I can make fathers stop drinking. I can make mothers stay." (p.10)

"Children can forgive their parents almost anything. It is one of those mysteries of life that no matter how badly a parent treats a child, somewhere in that child is a desperate need to forgive, a desperate need to be loved." (p. 47)

"I really had not expected very much happiness for my life. Children who suffer great loss often grow up believing deep inside that life is supposed to be hard for them. They sometimes don't know how to find comfort and a life that doesn't hurt. Once I learned to do this, I was able to make better decisions in everything because I carefully chose only those people and places which offered me peacefulness and love.

"I also had a little boy of my own when I grew up, and having a child helped me understand how scary it is to be somebody's parent, because you're always afraid you might screw things up for him.. I would like my son to have an easier childhood than mine.

"But every child will have his heartaches. I just hope that along with these each child will have a hero, and music, and at least one kiss he will never forget." (p. 53-54)

*Cynthia Rylant from* I'll Be Back Again

## Try this:

- *For 2–3 minutes, write as quickly as you can all that this piece of writing brings to mind for you.*

- *Looking at one of these excerpts, write as quickly as you can for 2–3 minutes all that comes to mind for you from that specific passage.*

Scholastic Professional Books    *100 Quickwrites* by Linda Rief

# I'd Rather...

I'd rather be locked in a cage with 47 lions, and a slab of meat tied to my back, than write.

I'd rather be sat on by a sumo wrestler than write.

I'd rather be hit in the head by a wrecking ball than write.

I'd rather wrestle a grizzly bear or get poked in the head by woodpeckers than write.

*Adam B.*

## Try this:

- *Look at Adam's cartoons and captions. Think about something you hate to do. Then think about things you would rather have happen to you. For 2–3 minutes, write as many as you can, as specifically as you can: "I'd rather _____ than _____."*

Scholastic Professional Books    *100 Quickwrites* by Linda Rief

# Available Light

I'll tell you
who I write for—the house
    plants—
outside all summer;
now, first frost, cloistered
in calm, indoor weather,
    especially
the geranium.

As leggy as any chorus line
    dancer
it kicks up and up
for whatever difference
one inch makes
in its proximity
to sun.

All that stretching and then
half its leaves
grow gold, drop, as I stoke
the woodstove, layer
myself in sweaters the color
of fire.
I've been told
repeatedly

by nursery people
geraniums won't keep over
    winter

unless you hang them
upside down in newspaper hoods
in a dark cellar.
As a child,

for punishment, I was made
to stand for hours
in a black stairwell corner
to consider my ill temper
but I knew those walls
were honeycombed
with treasure—

bracelets of Egyptian gold,
red-handled jump ropes, turtles
who could swallow whole lakes
and I used my time
standing in the dark
figuring ways to rescue

what was rightfully
mine. October, I place
the geranium
in the brightest window
I can find
where it shapes itself
to available light
and stays alive.

*Mekeel McBride from* Red Letter Days

## Try this:

- *For 2–3 minutes, write as quickly as you can all that this poem brings to mind for you.*
- *Borrow any line and write as quickly and as specifically as you can, letting the line lead your thinking.*
- *Write as quickly and as specifically as you can from the line "I'll tell you who I write for . . ."*

Scholastic Professional Books    *100 Quickwrites* by Linda Rief

# Eleanor Paine

When Rhonda read one of her poems in class
I sat there amazed
By a sensitivity I didn't know she possessed.
Isn't it enough for her to be beautiful?
She talks to boys as easily as if they were her brothers.
She plays tennis as though she were training for Wimbledon.
She tells jokes like a professional comedienne.
A week later, while sitting in the dentist's office,
I saw her poem in a magazine.
Only it didn't have her name on it.
I don't understand.
Why when she has everything
Does she want even more?

*Mel Glenn from* Class Dismissed!

## Try this:

- *For 2–3 minutes, write as quickly as you can all that this poem brings to mind for you.*
- *Borrow any line and write as quickly and specifically as you can, letting the line lead your thinking.*
- *What do you think about what Rhonda did? Write as quickly as you can.*

Scholastic Professional Books    *100 Quickwrites* by Linda Rief

# After English Class

I used to like "Stopping by Woods on a Snowy Evening."
I liked the coming darkness,
The jingle of harness bells, breaking—and adding to
     —the stillness,
The gentle drift of snow. . . .

But today, the teacher told us what everything stood for.
The woods, the horse, the miles to go, the sleep—
They all have "hidden meanings."

It's grown so complicated now that,
Next time I drive by,
I don't think I'll bother to stop.

*Jean Little from* Hey World, Here I Am!

## Try this:

- *For 2–3 minutes, write as quickly as you can all that this poem brings to mind for you.*
- *Borrow any line and write as quickly and as specifically as you can, letting the line lead your thinking.*

Scholastic Professional Books    *100 Quickwrites* by Linda Rief

# Reading

When I read I get pulled into another world. When I am there I am not there to watch, compare, and observe everything else in other worlds. When I read that is the only thing I know. When I read I am living that life. Maybe that's why I don't like to write responses to the books I'm reading. I like to write responses to the lives I'm living. . . .

*Juliana M.*

They say books take you to a far-away land. Hmmm. Not me. If that were true, then any book I like to read would scare me. Let's face it, six foot tall men rushing at us to dismember us would scare us, especially if those men are armorclad and waving deadly long swords that could sever my head in a swipe. I personally would not really care if I had "good King Richard" beside me. Books aren't like that. They show the scene and what's happening, but a part of you knows it is all right. You are not in the middle of the battle where your life expectancy will be greatly decreased. You are in your room and your life is comfortably out of danger. I personally like it that way. . . .

*Ben R.*

## Try this:

- *For 2–3 minutes, describe as specifically as you can what reading is like for you and why it's that way.*
- *Borrow any line—one from Juliana (for example, "When I read I get pulled into another world. . . .") or one from Ben (for example, "They say books take you to a far-away land. . . .")—and write off that line as quickly as you can, letting the line lead your thinking.*

Scholastic Professional Books     *100 Quickwrites* by Linda Rief

# My Grandmother's Hair

When I was living in my grandmother's small white house in Cool Ridge, West Virginia, I loved to comb my grandmother's hair. I was a thin, blondheaded little girl, and I would climb up on the back of the couch where my grandmother was sitting, straddle her shoulders with my skinny six-year-old legs, and I would gently, most carefully, lift a lock of soft gray hair and make my little pink comb slide through it. This always quieted us both, slowed down our heartbeats, and we would sigh together and then I would lift up another lock.

We talked of many things as I combed her fine hair. Our talk was quiet, and it had to do with those things we both knew about: cats, baking-powder biscuits, Sunday school class. Mrs. Epperly's big bull. Cherry picking. The striped red dress Aunt Violet sent me.

But we didn't always talk. Sometimes we were quiet. We would just think, and my small hands would move in my grandmother's hair, twirling, curling, rolling that soft grayness around. We thought about good things, the big clock in the living room ticking, and sometimes my grandmother would shiver and we laughed.

I often put bobby pins in her hair, made pin curls with them, and the rest of the morning or afternoon my grandmother would wear these pin curls I had made. Later, I'd watch as she stood before her mirror, taking them out one by one, and her gray locks would be tight as bedsprings and would dance if you pulled on them. But when she brushed through these tight little wads of curl, her hair became magic and grew and covered her face like a lion's mane.

I thought many times that I might grow up to be a hairdresser, twirling ladies' gray locks into magic curls and watching their faces light up as they saw themselves change.

But I became a writer instead. And used my little pink comb, and got quiet, and thought good thoughts, and twirled and curled and rolled words into good stories. The stories became books, and with the same hands I had once combed her hair with, I handed these books to my grandmother and watched as she turned the pages one by one, the big clock in the living room ticking.

Sometimes she shivered and we laughed.

There are many ways to learn to be a writer.

*Cynthia Rylant from* To Ride a Butterfly

## Try this:

- *For 2–3 minutes, write as quickly as you can all that this piece of writing brings to mind for you.*
- *Think of a person you are, or have been, close to and write as quickly and as specifically as you can for 2–3 minutes, all that comes to mind that you did with, and learned from, that person.*
- *Write as quickly and as specifically as you can in response to the line "There are many ways to learn to be a writer."*

Scholastic Professional Books  *100 Quickwrites* by Linda Rief

# The Unwritten Pages

I know
That somewhere
Are the words that remain invisible
They would love to sing
But they have no voice
They would love to breathe
But they have no air
So they wander
Unheard
Like music without a staff
And I know
Sometime
I will find those words
Help them sing and help them breathe
My pen will no longer remain still
My soul no longer
Unwritten

*Megan G.*

## Try this:

- *For 2–3 minutes, write as quickly as you can all that Megan's words bring to mind for you.*
- *Borrow any line and write as quickly and as specifically as you can, letting the line lead your thinking.*

Scholastic Professional Books     *100 Quickwrites* by Linda Rief

# Building From the Quickwrites

Quickwrites begin the thinking, letting students know they do have ideas and that they can get those ideas on paper. The quick, short jottings allow students to discover things they didn't know they knew before they started writing. Once they feel competent at finding their ideas, students begin to realize the power writing has to help them develop more deeply and fully as thinkers.

After these initial thoughts or ideas or feelings are captured, what happens? How do students go beyond these first efforts? Writing is a recursive process through which writers find, develop, re-see, craft, and refine their ideas. It takes time. The writing process gives writers the chance to shape their ideas for a specific audience and purpose. This too takes time.

In contrast to the short burst of writing that plants the seed of an idea in a quickwrite, the nurturing phase in which the idea comes to fruition can last for days, or weeks, or even months. This book is meant to be a collection of models that inspire students to capture their thoughts and words on paper, but in this section I want to explain briefly some of the ways I work with my students to help their initial writings grow into fuller, more developed pieces over time.

## Where to Collect the Quickwrites: Keeping a Reader's-Writer's Notebook (or Journal)

My students date their quickwrites and write them in the response section of their Reader's-Writer's Notebook. In addition to the quickwrites, they write or draw in response to their required half hour of nightly reading, and they collect any ideas they have for writing. The quickwrites they do several times a week count toward the three to five pages of writing I require in this response section each week. (This amount of writing is individualized and modified based on prior experience with the students and what they and I, working together, believe makes sense to keep them growing as readers and writers. All students are not at the same place at the same time.)

### Benefit of Collecting

Keeping these initial ideas in one place—rather than on separate sheets of paper that have a tendency to vanish in bottomless lockers—allows students to collect them, look back on them, and reconsider their value. It also allows me to see what students have written and to prompt further thinking and writing when I offer my response. Still, quickwrites are first drafts, and the decision to simply collect and save them or to develop them remains with the students.

# Responding to the Quickwrites

When I collect students' notebooks every two weeks (one section of approximately 25 students on Monday, another section on Tuesday, and so forth), I read through them and respond in a variety of ways, depending on the writing and the students' needs. In the section below, I describe how I responded—or did not respond—to specific pieces.

## Some Quickwrites Remain Undeveloped

Quickwrites may remain undeveloped in the notebook, with neither the student choosing to say any more, nor me providing any comments. At a minimum, their thinking is recorded. Students still get credit for this writing, even as it remains in just the notebook or journal.

Hilda seldom develops any of her quickwrites into anything lengthier or fuller. She is thinking and playing with language every time she writes. In a quickwrite in response to a winter poem, Hilda wrote:

*I'm really tired of winter poems. I know the look and feel and thoughts of snow falling around me. I know the night feeling of dirty slush and streetlights. I know that the sun abandons us earlier and earlier and the bite of cold stings into my skin. I know the warmth of a hug in the blazing chill and how empty trees scrape the sky. I know all of this. I live it. I don't need the constant reminders that this is winter.*

In a two-minute response to an excerpt from *Sitti's Secrets* by Naomi Shihab Nye she wrote:

*I hate prejudices. I hate that whispered things and glances would build up so much that a <u>girl with cinnamon skin</u> would raise her hand and say "I wish there was no such things as homosexuality." This hurts, as the only 'out' person in our middle school. I wish that we didn't have that kind of feeling in our classrooms, these pent up feelings of distance. 'Gay Youth' is just a term that means people outside of our schools, our towns, our states. <u>Wrong.</u> <u>We need to educate the people in our halls</u> and classrooms that these are real people. This term that seems so distant is really people walking our streets, working in our stores. These are people you could sit with on the bus, maybe even your friends, neighbors, family.*

Two weeks later, Hilda wrote quickly in response to a passage about the cutting of hair in *The Giver* by Lois Lowry:

*I remember that night, <u>late darkness through melted windows</u> and <u>the weight of my hair pressing into my head</u> more and more. This is something you've always wanted to do, I'm thinking. <u>Why wait any longer?</u> And <u>I am cutting it off. Bundles of thick hair—black dye and blonde roots. I am pushing heavy black-handled scissors</u> through my long, thick hair. <u>I am cutting</u> as close to my scalp as I can. <u>I am feeling</u> the freedom of air on my scalp. Small hairs stick on my neck, and my face seems somehow distorted in the old mirror, sharp edges and divots in shortened hair.*

*I like the rhythm created by the repetition of "I am."*

---

> **What can we expect students to do with these quickwrites?**
>
> - *Simply collect and save them for future reference*
> - *Expand on them right away or later with further ideas*
> - *Take to peers and teachers for feedback on content*
> - *Re-see, redraft into more polished pieces*
> - *Take to final drafts of best writing*

Hilda's stance in the first quickwrite—that she doesn't want any more reminders of winter—tells me she is done with this line of thinking, and I decide not to push her to tell me more about all she doesn't like, or does like, about winter poems or winter. I could ask her to tell me about the season she does like most. What are the sights and sounds and smells and moments of that season? But since she's an accomplished writer who has no trouble choosing her own topics, I do not prompt her further.

In reference to the second quickwrite, I could ask Hilda to tell me more about her own experiences with prejudice and how she thinks we can better educate people. Since I know she will when she's ready, I do not write anything.

In the few months school has been in session I have watched Hilda's hairstyles change dramatically—from shaved head to mohawk, from blonde to green to purple. Her hair fascinates me. I could write, *Tell me more about how you change your hair and why,* but I don't. In the same way she plays with her hairstyles, she uses the quickwrites to play with her thinking and with language. These pieces often lead to deeper, much more detailed and complex pieces that bear a resemblance to the quickwrites. I can see where the seeds of ideas were planted. I give her credit for the writing, but ask her little else in this or in many of her quickwrites, as she seldom answers me. She already knows where she's headed. The quickwrites just put her in the driver's seat. I do, however, underline strong images, or ideas I suspect she could say more about. I often put brackets or stars next to specific quickwrites that pique my interest. Students know these are the possibilities they might return to.

James wrote in response to "The Game" by Myra Cohn Livingston (p. 101):

 *this peace of poetry reminds me of the war were going into, and how bad the out come can and probably will turn out horribly, but on a lighter note. It also reminds me all the fighting video games I have. I don't think war is the answer to anything but games like James bond and perfect dark, are my favorite games and I think as long as you can tell the difference between games and life it's ok because when you kill someone they don't just push start and start over.*

I starred this entry when I read his journal and wrote,

*You really see the seriousness of life situations as opposed to games. Tell me more about the difference between video games and real war. In what ways are they similar? In what ways are they different? Some people think kids can't tell the difference between video games and real life. What do you think? Do you think playing too many of these games affects kids? In what ways?*

James had not yet expanded on this writing, but should he have nothing to write about one day, this quickwrite and my questions might suggest a topic. James might have something to say about the notion that some people believe playing too many video games leads to violent behavior. He knows the difference between real life and games and might have a strong opinion about that stance. It's an idea worth pursuing, and my questions are meant to nudge him to consider the possibilities embedded in this initial thinking.

It's important to note that this is first-draft thinking, and I seldom correct the spelling or the punctuation. Students are asked to write fast to capture their thoughts. Conventions of language don't count in this first draft writing.

## Expanding on the Quickwrite

Sometimes students have a lot more to say about an issue even without my prompting, and they simply continue writing on their initial idea, either in their notebook or on separate sheets of paper, during writing time.

In response to "Black River" by Janet (p. 87), Emily wrote:

> *This reminds me of Christmas this year. There was a huge snowstorm that day, more snow than we had gotten for the whole winter last year. My best friend's family came over for Christmas dinner, battling their way through the thickening storm. We spent the afternoon eating and talking about presents, occasionally glancing outdoors at the white world outside. But once darkness had fallen we decided that we wanted to go sledding on the hill in my backyard. Realizing that neither of us had sledded since sixth grade, we became fixed on this goal. <u>Our parents finally gave in,</u> and we headed outside . . . (she ended the quickwrite here, but during writing time went back and added more) . . . The <u>whole world</u> was <u>buried in snow.</u> The <u>dead reeds at the bottom of the slope</u> are <u>usually clacking in the breeze,</u> but that night their <u>sound was dampened by flakes.</u> The snow was a <u>fogged-over mirror,</u> gently <u>reflecting an orange light</u> from the neighbor's house. <u>Icy pellets</u> falling from the smoky sky fogged Cassie's glasses and stung my eyes. Frozen, my hands wet and numb, I mounted the sled and began to move downhill, a <u>deep drift of snow piling in front of me.</u>*
>
> *It took several minutes for the path to smooth out. By then I was shivering with cold, <u>ice water in my veins</u>. But <u>after just one run down the hill, all that was forgotten. What could be better, I now wonder, than sledding in a blizzard on Christmas night?</u>*

When I read Emily's notebook for the two-week period, I underlined the lines from this quickwrite that I especially liked for their sense of sight, sound, and feel. I also liked the way she ended this with a question that needed no answer. So far this writing has not gone any further. I haven't suggested to Emily to take it any further because she has plenty of drafts of writing that she is already working on. This piece has potential should she become stuck; I'm wondering how they wheedled their parents to let them sled. By underlining certain lines, I suggest places where she might find some ideas, should she be looking.

A powerful quickwrite model is "Bullfrogs" by David Allen Evans (from *Poetspeak*), a poem in which young people cut off the legs of frogs and throw the bodies into the water—and then look back and see the eyes staring at them. When Amy listened to "Bullfrogs" she wrote down the final line, "asking for their legs" and continued with

> *This made me think of Petey, a man with cerebral palsy. He could never walk and was always contained in either a bed and then when he got luckier, a wheelchair. I wonder if he ever asked for his legs, asked for strong legs, to let him walk. He had legs that bent in at the knees and were shriveled, weak and useless. I wonder if he ever wished for his legs.*

Several days later in her Reader's-Writer's Notebook she wrote:

*I enjoyed the book* Petey (Ben Mikaelsen) *for several reasons:*

1. *It made me try to imagine my life if I could not walk or talk effectively. That would be so hard.*

2. *It made me try to imagine never really being independent, always having to rely on someone else to care for me.*

3. *It gave me great glimpses of the potential the human mind has, regardless of how the body works. You'll always have your thoughts, dreams, observations.*

4. *This book deepened my respect for people with disabilities. I guess I had never stopped to think and imagine what life must be like for them.*

5. *It also made me more conscious of how people act around others with disabilities. I will try to do as Trevor did—to get over the initial reactions I may have and not be turned off by appearances or what may seem to be a lack of intelligence, thought and life. People who can not speak may be dying to tell their stories. They may just need someone to learn their language.*

Quickwrites often lingered in Emily's mind and reentered her notebook in different forms throughout the year—a list, a poem, questions, an opinion, a letter, an essay. Every time she wrote it was to further her thinking by taking herself back to push herself forward. I had only starred that first entry, telling her that her words were worth listening to, poignant, and provocative to my thinking.

## Nudging an Idea

When I read a quickwrite that I think holds potential for a lot more thinking, I might simply star or bracket that writing *and* jot a note in the student's notebook:

- *Tell me more,* or
- *This is really interesting. What happened? Tell me more,* or
- *This creates a vivid picture in my mind. Tell me more,* or
- *You really feel strongly about that. Tell me more.*

It is difficult to say exactly what questions nudge a writer further, but I've found that honestly responding and asking a student to "tell me more" shows enough interest to elicit more writing, from which even more questions and suggestions may evolve.

Ryan responded to Lindsay's poem about her grandmother (see page 64) by borrowing her first line, "I remember we . . ." and wrote for two minutes in his journal.

*I remember we went to the fair and you brought me on all the scary rides, and all the bonfires we had on the beach as we watched the day go by and how you told me stories, the best I've ever heard.*

In my reading of his notebook at the end of two weeks, I starred this quickwrite and said I liked the detail of particular events. I wrote, *Who are you doing these things with? Tell me more.* Because he knew he needed two final drafts of writing, and had only one other piece started, he read his quickwrite to a friend and ended up adding several more lines when she asked, "What else did you do together?" He wrote a second draft:

*I Remember . . .*

*I remember when you took me to the fair and brought me on all the scary rides.*
*And all the bonfires we had on the beach as we watched the day go by.*
*And how you always told me stories, the best I've ever heard.*
*And how you always offered me popsicles, saying one was just obserd.*
*And when you came to my football games, you always cheered me on.*
*And then you brought me home, and played catch with me on the lawn.*
*And how you always cracked a joke, even at the toughest times.*
*And how you had so much wisdom to share, the funniest ones would rhyme.*
*And I remember all the plane rides home, when I only thought of you,*
*Thinking of the things we did, and the things that we will do.*

Ryan read this draft to me and showed me how he had set up the lines and the rhyming. I pointed out again how much his love for his grandfather came through in each detail. I suggested he consider moving "and" from the second line to the end of the first line, and to consider using the other "ands" a bit more sparingly to give the eye a break—perhaps every other line and perhaps an odd number of times to give the ear a bit more variety in sound. He added "Pappy" to his title and switched the endings of lines seven and eight around to make more sense. I gave him the correct spelling for "absurd."

This became a poem he liked a lot and couldn't wait to send to his grandfather; see the final version.

*I Remember . . . Pappy . . .*

*When you took me to the fair and brought me on all the scary rides. And*
*All the bonfires we had on the beach as we watched the day go by.*
*And how you always told me stories, the best I've ever heard.*
*How you always offered me Popsicles, saying one was just absurd.*
*And when you came to my football games, you always cheered me on.*
*Then you brought me home, and played catch with me on the lawn.*
*You always cracked a joke, the funniest ones would rhyme.*
*You always had so much wisdom to share, even at the toughest times.*
*And I remember all the plane rides home, when I only thought of you,*
*Thinking of the things we did, and the things that we will do.*

I nudged Katie in a similar way, with checks next to details she included in a quickwrite she did in response to my rambling autobiography (see page 30). I told the students to write their own autobiography, thinking especially of the things they did when they were little. Katie wrote:

*Children run through sprinklers on a sticky summer day, you hit your first*
*home run in T-ball with that special boy watching from the stands,*
*sandcastles tower over small children's faces and watermelon juice dripping*
*down your cheeks, you play hide 'n seek in clothes racks and jumping from*
*rocks into the deep blue sea of the ocean, you listen patiently for the music*
*of the ice cream truck . . .*

In two minutes this is as much as she was able to write. During writing time she added another page and a half of things children do—or more likely, that she did.

She said she liked what she had written and asked to read the first draft to me. I repeated back to her the lines that stuck with me, the ones that were the strongest images and feelings of childhood. I suggested she think about using the present tense throughout, as if she were still living these rambling events, and that even the use of the second person "you" would help pull the reader into the moments. I left her with the question, *Could you think of an ending that surprises the reader as well as surprises the child in this piece? Think about how quickly time passes.*

Katie worked on the piece for several days and ended up with:

> *On a sticky summer day you run through sprinklers, hit your first homerun in T-ball, and build sandcastles while watermelon juice drips down your cheeks. You play hide'n seek in clothes racks, listen patiently for the music of the ice cream truck with puffy eyes from swimming in a teal-blue public pool. You crawl through homemade blanket forts and roll huge snow balls for your first snowman. You dress up in fancy sparkling gowns and high heels three sizes too big. You draw your name in the sand and watch it wash away with the tide. You catch fireflies in jars to light up the night, fall back into freshly fallen snow to make a snow angel. And you finally make it down your driveway without training wheels, and cannon ball into a mountain of red and orange and yellow leaves. On Christmas Eve you cuddle in front of a fireplace to see if Santa really comes. You tuck your first doll into her crib before desperately trying to blow out all five candles on your birthday cake and suddenly realize there are fourteen.*

Katie liked the ending. She never took this to a final draft of best writing, as she didn't feel it was one of her stronger pieces. It still had, and has, the potential to be crafted into an even stronger piece. The initial ideas are here. She might think more about the sights, and sounds, and smells of her childhood and reorganize some of the details into a pattern that shows some vague connection as she moves from one recollection to the next. The ending is a wonderfully subtle way of showing the passage of time in the same way it shocks the child.

Ben wrote little throughout the year. It took him until spring to actually produce much writing. I always invite students to use quick sketches instead of writing if that comes more easily to them. Ben drew in response to my writing about being young at the ocean (see page 37). I read to the students and then asked them to write about or sketch a place they loved going or hated going when they were younger. Ben drew himself at the ocean and then wrote:

> *(This is a) picture of me sitting on the beach watching the waves crash on the shorline like big rocks bashing against each other. I did this drawing because I think I was scared of the beach when I was little and watching every one having so much fun. I also had another problem. I was fat and very scared if I touck my sheart off I would be teased like when I'm in school.*

I didn't read this piece until I read Ben's notebook at the two-week point. In response I wrote: *This is a great description—the beach is not a soothing place in this memory. What scared you about the beach? The picture brought out strong feelings and words. This is beautifully written, almost poetry. Here's how you might start shaping this into a poem:*

| | |
|---|---|
| *I am five.* | *Big rocks bashing* |
| *I am sitting on the beach* | *Against each other.* |
| *Watching waves crash* | *I am five and* |
| *On the shoreline like* | *I am scared. . .* |

Even with my suggestions, Ben could not understand how to continue crafting his thinking as a poem or in any other format. He had said what he needed to say, I understood the feeling, and he was satisfied with the way he said it. He had taken great risk admitting his fear. This was a big step toward writing for him, telling the truth and reliving the experience.

Sometimes we have to let the ideas we recognize as potential in a student's work go. Even if they do not recognize the same possibilities that we do, their accomplishment is still compelling.

## Encouraging Students to Take Quickwrites to a Well-Developed Draft

Juliana used two quickwrite jottings to craft a piece about her great-uncle's barbershop. In October she wrote a quickwrite in response to the poem "Barbers" from Cynthia Rylant's book *Something Permanent*. She wrote one paragraph in response to "Barbers." But the minute she was given time to continue writing on any piece of her choice, she went right back to this piece and wrote several more pages.

Several months later I had the students respond to the passage about the cutting of hair in Lois Lowry's *The Giver*. Juliana went back to her first quickwrite. She already had a first draft of the piece in her journal. Her memories flooded back the more she wrote, and she wanted to capture as much of her thinking as she could.

I had starred and bracketed this initial piece of writing. She knew it had potential. She read it to several peers and to me to find out what was working and what she needed to expand. We pointed out the lines that let us see and hear and smell that barber shop. We asked her questions, some of which she answered. Over several months the piece moved from one paragraph to this longer piece. She used the passage from *The Giver* (Lowry, p.46) about hair as an epigraph; then she wrote:

> *My great-uncle Pete has a barbershop. Every time I step into that room it's like going back in time. There is a striped barber's pole, comfy leather chairs, and black and white photos covering the walls. As my brother's hair is being cut, my father points to the people in the pictures. "That's Nana and her brothers. That's me with Mary Jean. That's one of Johnnie's paintings." Johnnie was the artist/photographer of the family. I have a huge extended family. Sometimes people will come into the shop. My father calculates in his head and then says something like, "This is your fourth cousin, twice removed," and I shake hands with this distant relative I've never seen in my life.*
>
> *On the wall is one big painting of Johnnie's. It is of Scilla, the town from which every member of my dad's family is descended. Scilla is in Italy, at the very toe of the boot. The ocean is bright blue and all the streets are neatly lined with rows of quaint little houses roofed with red tiles. Cliffs hang over the water and white wave caps crash on the shore. It's a beautiful painting.*

*I never had the chance to meet Johnnie, but his paintings have inspired me to try to be an artist like he is. He drew Scilla from photographs and stories, but never from real life. If I ever go to Scilla I will sit on those cliffs and paint.*

*The rest of the wall is covered with a scattered arrangement of other memories. The photographs have torn corners and are all of old or deceased relatives standing in front of the old family barbershop. The men all have their hair slicked back and are wearing white crisp uniforms with old-fashioned square caps. All the women are in long dark dresses with little dogs in their arms and smiles on their faces. There are newer photographs also, of little babies, of anniversaries, and 80th birthday celebrations.*

*The barber's chair sits in the middle of the room on a brown rubber mat. The mirror is spotted. A cluster of spray bottles and combs and scissors in jars of green liquid are lying scattered around a small table.*

*My great-uncle is over ninety and has gone through several major surgeries that he was only half-expected to survive. He always wears an old camel barber shirt and brown corduroy pants. His gray hair is thin, but always combed neatly. His dark hands are freckled with sunspots and moles and they are rough and muscular from his work. He holds his plain metal barber scissors firmly in his hand, twisting his whole arm as he carves out hairstyles. He takes a break from cutting, to examine his handy work or check if the bangs are coming out even; he continues to snap his scissors, cutting through the air. Scrape, click, scrape, click.*

*While he goes through the motions, hair cascades to the brown rubber mat and he talks. His stories are engrossing even though I've heard them all before. There is a pattern to his speech, and wisdom to his words. He talks about things he did yesterday or seventy years ago and you can hardly tell the difference.*

*I fidget in the chair as he sweeps up my brother's fallen hair. He starts the story of his heart bypass surgery from a few years ago. "I was there outside the operating room on a table . . . you know the ones they wheel you around on? I'd told Aunt Mary and the kids that I loved them, and then they wheel me into the operating room and before they give me the medicine so I sleep, the doctor tells me, 'Peter, you need to understand that there are three possible outcomes of this surgery. You could just die right here on the operating table. You could end up bleeding to death, or it could turn out fine.' So I look at him and say, 'Do I get a choice?' He laughs and the other doctor says, 'I'm ready,' and I say, 'I am also.' Then the Doc says, 'I'm going to count backward from ten and then you'll fall asleep.' And then he starts counting '10 . . . 9 . . .' you know? But I'm not counting, I'm praying and asking Him to be with my family and then the next thing I know I'm awake and the doctor's telling me it went well. 'Johnny, you know,' he says to my father, 'the doctors thought I shouldn't have heart surgery at my age but Rockie—remember Rockie Lofaro, Johnny? He's a doctor now—he says, 'treat this man like he's sixty.' That's what he told them, Johnny."*

*My Uncle Pete has faith and selflessness I've not seen matched by anyone. He has a very trusting outlook on life. He believes God is always there to help and guide everyone, and even though that's not what I believe, in the same sense, I see that God is there for him. He is the kind of man who I*

*can never imagine dead. He will always be there in his barber shop, cutting*
*hair, recalling his past and saying in his typical old Italian accent, "No,*
*Johnny . . . I couldn't . . ." with a wave of his hand, when my father offers*
*to pay him.*

This is such a beautiful piece of writing because Juliana has pulled us in close to one man, one family, one human being, in one setting—through meticulous observation and careful listening. Through her vivid narrative, we have a poignant view of all that makes us human. She teaches us about process by showing us how she goes back to quickwrites, to a novel she read, to responses in her notebook, and then uses an extended period of time and redrafting to combine her ideas. She teaches us craft lessons by weaving together narration, description, and dialogue. Her carefully chosen words walk us around the barbershop so we can see and hear and care about Uncle Pete. She helps us think about family—our family—through her family. Even Juliana's well-crafted ending suggests the humility of the man, the simplicity of his life, and the poignancy of E.B. White's admonition to writers: "Write about *a* man, not man." Juliana does it all so well.

## Developing a Piece to Its Fullest Potential: Teaching Through Conferences

At the heart of moving writing forward is feedback from listeners. My students get responses from their peers as well as from me. I teach the students a particular way to respond to each other because I've learned this is the kind of response that pushes me forward as a writer. I ask my students at the eighth-grade level to bring two pieces of writing to final draft every four weeks, and it is for these pieces that students schedule conferences, first with their peers and then with me.

Before I ask students to respond to each others' writing, I model how I want them to do so with my own writing. I put a draft of something I'm writing on the overhead projector. I ask students to listen carefully to my piece as I read it to them from the screen. I give each of them a conference sheet that says:

- You can help me by _____ .
- Tell me what phrases you hear, like, are surprised by, or that stick with you (that I wrote).
- What questions come to mind (as I read to you)?
- What's one suggestion you could give me (based on what I asked for as help)?

This structure helps the students stay focused on the writing they are listening to and to offer the kinds of comments that will make the writing better. Stating right away how listeners can help the writer focuses the listeners on what the writer has already perceived as the most problematic area for which he or she wants, and therefore welcomes, help. Listeners must write these phrases, questions, and suggestions down as they are listening to the piece being read to them, so they don't forget what they were thinking.

Repeating phrases or sections back to the writer tells her that she was heard, that the language or construction affected the listener in some way, and that these might be the areas the writer wants to preserve. As I model this with my own writing,

I put check marks next to the phrases the students repeat back to me (in response to the second prompt above).

Questions from listeners tell writers the information that they might consider adding. Then writers must ask themselves, *Is it important to add that? How many listeners had the same questions? What questions seem relevant to answer?* I model this thinking with my students' responses to my own writing.

Listeners' suggestions should be focused on the areas the writer perceives as needing help. Did the writer want a stronger title? A more compelling lead? An ending that kept the listener guessing? More detail for the character? More convincing arguments? Was the writer wondering about tense? Or person? Or change in time? How could the writer make the character more believable? Would this work better as poetry or prose?

This is the structure students must follow as they respond to each other whether the writer is sharing with the whole class, a small group, or one person. It is the structure that I have found that best helps the writer craft his or her ideas. Generic response—"That was good," "That was interesting"—is no help at all. This structure also prevents negative response, such as "You have a weak lead" or "There's no point to this," which is not constructive criticism and only makes the writer defensive, holding more tightly to his first draft.

Approximately half of the writing the students choose to take to a final draft comes from quickwrites. I take one or more of my quickwrites that I want to develop further to whole class conferences with the students. I model several pieces like this before I ask them to take writing of theirs to a small group or before they read it to me. Students always read their own writing in a conference when they are working to revise it. I want them to be responsible for hearing their own voices as they write, revise, and edit.

## Re-looking at the Models

Any one of the models included in this book can be re-looked at a second or third time to help the students gain insight about leads, endings, line breaks, use of punctuation, titles, layers of meaning, fragments, writer's intentions, word choices, and so on. The possibilities for using the models to explore craft elements are virtually limitless.

One of the things I point out specifically to students, especially when we re-look at these models and re-look at their own quickwrites in response to them, is that they no longer need a line they may have borrowed. In the process of crafting an initial quickwrite to a more finished draft, they can get rid of a borrowed line that prompted the quickwrite. If they choose to keep a line from one of the models—whether it is a first line, a repeated line, an embedded line, an ending, or an epigraph—then I show them how to put that line in italics to indicate it came from someone else's writing.

---

Over the last thirty years there have been many books published that describe the writing workshop, especially for adolescents, in much deeper detail. I have listed only some of these books in the references and recommend reading these resources for a deeper understanding of the complexities of the writing process.

Don Murray says that good writing makes us think *or* feel something; the best writing makes us think *and* feel something. So many of the students whose writing is in this collection didn't think they had anything to say. Giving them another student's words to hold on to, until they found their own, gave them the confidence to know they could show us what they think and feel.

# Professional References

Atwell, Nancie. *Lessons That Change Writers*. Portsmouth, NH: Heinemann, 2002.

——. *In the Middle: New Understandings About Writing, Reading, and Learning*. Portsmouth, NH: Boynton/Cook, 1998.

Elbow, Peter. *Writing with Power: Techniques for Mastering the Writing Process*. New York: Oxford University Press, 1981.

Fletcher, Ralph. *What a Writer Needs*. Portsmouth, NH: Heinemann, 1993.

Fletcher, Ralph and Joann Portalupi. *Craft Lessons: Teaching Writing K-8*. York, Maine: Stenhouse, 1998.

——. *Nonfiction Craft Lessons: Teaching Information Writing K-8*. York, Maine: Stenhouse, 2001.

——. *Writing Workshop: The Essential Guide*. Portsmouth, NH: Heinemann, 2001.

Graves, Donald. *A Fresh Look at Writing*. Portsmouth, NH: Heinemann, 1994.

Kaufman, Douglas. *Conferences and Conversations: Listening to the Literate Classroom*. Portsmouth, NH: Heinemann, 2000.

Lane, Barry. *After the End: Teaching and Learning Creative Revision*. Portsmouth, NH: Heinemann, 1993.

Murray, Donald M. *The Craft of Revision*. Fort Worth: Harcourt Brace, 1995.

——. *A Writer Teaches Writing*. Boston: Houghton Mifflin, 1990.

Rief, Linda. *Seeking Diversity: Language Arts with Adolescents*. Portsmouth, NH: Heinemann, 1992.

——. *Vision and Voice: Extending the Literacy Spectrum*. Portsmouth, NH: Heinemann, 1998.

Romano, Tom. *Writing with Passion: Life Stories, Multiple Genres*. Portsmouth, NH: Boynton-Cook, 1995.

*For professional sources of quickwrite models, see page 116.*